CHANGE YOUR ATTITUDE...
CHANGE YOUR LIFE

KEYS TO A GOOD LIFE

WISDOM TO
UNLOCK YOUR
POWER WITHIN

CHANGE YOUR ATTITUDE...CHANGE YOUR LIFE

KEYS TO A GOOD LIFE

WISDOM TO UNLOCK YOUR POWER WITHIN

Maximilian Publishing, LLC
December 2015

Notice
This book is intended as a reference volume only. The information
provided is the opinion of each contributor and is not intended
as a substitute for advice from a professional who knows your
personal situation.

Mention of specific companies, organizations, or authorities in
this book does not imply endorsement by the publisher, nor does
mention of specific companies, organizations, or authorities imply
that they endorse this book.

Printed in the United States of America

ISBN 978-0-9897232-1-3
Maximilian Publishing, LLC

CONTENTS

INTRODUCTION

When I created the Change Your Attitude…Change Your Life (CYACYL) brand six years ago, it was my mission to empower people through education. My work is based on the philosophy of Francis Bacon who said that knowledge is power, and I have been striving to educate, inspire, and motivate others using multiple mediums including radio, magazine publishing, and public speaking. A book is the next step in the blueprint of my vision.

In keeping with my desire to be a conduit of information, I assembled a group of experts to create a publication that would address everyday issues. From stress reduction to professional development to improved health and well-being, contributors share stories, ideas, and insights to help guide you through your personal life journey.

KEYS TO A GOOD LIFE: *Wisdom to Unlock Your Power Within*, is a collaboration of life-changing information from people who have experienced transformation either through an outside circumstance or by an inward call for change. Each chapter consists of wisdom to help you live your best life possible.

I sincerely thank the contributors who have shared their creativity, knowledge, and skills, and I invite you to Change Your Attitude…Change Your Life.

Joan Herrmann
Radio Host, Author,
Publisher, Speaker

ANXIETY

Anxiety does not empty tomorrow of its sorrows,
but only empties today of its strength.
– Charles Spurgeon

CHAPTER 1

ANXIETY AND SEVEN WAYS TO OVERCOME IT

BY JUDE BIJOU, M.A., M.F.T.

Anxiety is a feeling. It shows up in our bodies and in our minds. Our muscles tighten, we can't breathe, our heart races. We think, "What if this happens?" "I can't handle this." "It's too much." "This will never end."

The emotion underlying anxiety is fear. Fear is a natural emotion when our survival feels threatened, whether it's our plane going through turbulence, our house being foreclosed, or a tornado ripping up our town. It also manifests in other ways – as nervous anxiety when your boss enters the room, worrying all night about an upcoming surgery or job interview, feeling too scattered to concentrate, or being lost and overwhelmed.

Before we learn how to handle anxiety, we need to understand emotions. According to Attitude Reconstruction, humans have six emotions – sadness, anger, fear, joy, love, and peace. These emotions are natural reactions to specific events, such as hurts and losses (sadness), violations and injustices (anger), threats to our safety (fear), accomplishments and beauty (joy), acts of kindness or giving (love), and feeling safe and secure (peace).

Regardless of how out of control or charged emotions seem, they're just pure energy. EMOTION = E + motion = energy + motion. There are no words. Emotions are just pure and distinct physical sensations in the body.

In addition, each of us was born with a dominant emotion that determines how we're likely to react in any situation. In other words, we're predisposed to process our minute-by-minute experience through a veil of sadness, anger, or fear and that, in turn, determines what we will feel, think, say, and do.

People whose dominant emotion is fear are easy to recognize. In general, they are the "speedy ones," focused on time, money, and getting things done. They think there's never enough time. They feel anxious, overwhelmed, paralyzed. Fear folks tend to be worriers – scattered, confused, dramatic, panicky, or controlling. They live in a nearly constant state of fight, flight, frenzy, or freeze. Peace is something that eludes them.

SEVEN WAYS TO HANDLE ANXIETY

If anxiety is a familiar experience, you're feeling fear. And if you're not expressing that emotional energy physically, naturally, and constructively, (like 98% of humans), the results are predictable: your attention resides in the future, entertaining all those "what ifs." You resort to global generalities such as "always" and "never." You lose sight of what is true or real, and you attempt to control.

You can control how you respond to those body sensations and fretful thoughts before they turn into disabling phobias. Anxiety and fear don't have to control your life. By incorporating some of the suggestions below, you'll restore balance, feel less anxiety, and increase the amount of time you feel peace – that is, calm, content, and relaxed yet alert.

1. Shiver the fear physiology out of your body rather than tightening up. Like a dog at the vet, or your body after an accident, when you feel anxious (fear), let your body do what's natural. Wiggle, jiggle, shudder, tremble, and quiver. Up the back. Out the arms, hands, and legs. In the neck and face. Ham it up. Put on music. This moves emotional energy out of your body so calm can be restored. Release the fear (even better when accompanied by eeek or brrrr) and feel the peace! However, this is key: while shivering, don't indulge in lumping and jumping about worst-case scenarios. Just remind yourself: "It's okay. I'm just feeling scared. I just need to shake."

As a side-note, if you can't sleep at night because of worry and "what ifs," get out of bed, and shiver, quiver, and shudder hard, for one or two minutes. Move that energy so both body and mind can settle, and you'll quickly fall asleep. It's almost magic. It's effective and it's free. However, while shivering don't indulge anxious thinking. Instead, keep telling yourself

"It's okay. I just feel fear. Everything will be all right. I'll handle this in the morning. Now is the time for sleep."

When anxiety goes unchecked for a long time, you may develop panic attacks. If you do, shiver when you feel it coming on. Let the energy move out of your body, while continuing to breathe and remind yourself that it is all okay, you are just feeling an emotion, and need to physically move the energy. Keep your eyes open and shake it out until calm is restored. Then you'll be able to get on with your day.

2. Vigilantly interrupt thoughts about the past or future, and any over-generalizations. The words "what if," "always," and "never" fuel fear. Replace these treacherous thoughts with statements about what is true right now.

Over and over, many times a day, think reassuring thoughts that restore perspective. Select two or three of the following truths. Then tenaciously interrupt all thoughts to the contrary by repeating what is true. Positive self-talk and reassurance really do change your attitude and pacify your body.

Thoughts about what's happening in your body:
This feeling is temporary.
This will pass.
Fear is normal.
It's just energy.
This won't kill me.
I still need to do or say this.

Peaceful thoughts about the reality:
Everything will be all right.
Everything is all right.
One thing at a time.
Be here now.
Stay specific.
Everything is unfolding in its own time.
I'll handle the future in the future.

3. Stay specific. When we're in the grip of fear, our mind catapults out of the present and into the past, future, fueled by dramatic overgeneralizations that only amplify and distort the situation at hand. Reel yourself back in by staying specific.

Bringing other unresolved issues into the topic at hand is like putting gasoline on the barbecue, and makes reaching a resolution nearly impossible. Stay in the present moment and deal with one thing at a time. Staying focused keeps things manageable.

For example, instead of thinking, "I'll never get all this handled," tell yourself, "Today I'll chip away at XYZ." Instead of saying, "My partner never follows through on promises he makes," address the single transgression and say, "I'd like to talk about the plan we made to meet for dinner at 6 p.m."

4. Make a list of what needs attention and handle one at a time. The key to managing anxiety about life's tasks is taking time daily to get organized. Write down all the things you need to do. Look at your list, prioritize the items, then focus on one thing at a time. Each step must be made small enough so you can do it. Put it in an obvious place so you can see it. Then just do what's next, keep your focus on the present, and offer yourself copious praise along the way.

5. Let go and say "no" more often to invitations of responsibility. Anxious folks have a tendency to believe that if they don't do it, it won't get done. This stems from their need to control in order to feel safe and to be liked or loved. Ironically, this strategy keeps you feeling anxious, over-stimulated, and overwhelmed. The world won't collapse if someone else does it their way. People don't abandon you. You'll still be a good person if you carve out time to do calming activities and let others take up the slack. Shiver and say, "No." Take a leisurely walk. Take a snooze.

6. Look within for the right action. Often, anxiety is just something in our minds that requires no action. But sometimes we can relieve the feeling by pausing and asking within for what action needs to be done. Maybe it's taking a "fear of flying" course, talking to your mate, asking your boss for help, or learning to meditate. Ask yourself if there's any action called for, and listen. Your heart will guide you well. If you can't hear, shake and shiver, then ask again.

7. Establish a regular, more relaxed routine and be mindful of what you eat, drink, and do. To feel calmer, you must reduce the amount of stimulation you're exposed to. That means spending time away from stressful and anxiety-producing activities, situations, movies, games, and other input. Hang out with safe, supportive people. Get more regular sleep. Don't miss meals. Cut down on the coffee and energy drinks. Avoid cold foods and drinks. Give yourself encouragement and reassurances. Keep offering praise for each small victory. You have a choice to beat yourself up or be your best friend. Say, "Good for me," or "I'm doing good."

By following these simple suggestions, you gain major ground in decreasing the amount of anxiety and fear that you feel. Shiver when you feel the fear in your body, remember what is really true, and break things into doable steps. Implement a couple of these tips each day. You'll feel more relaxed and at peace while handling what's presented more flexibly and creatively. You'll enjoy whatever your day brings and willingly participate with humor and equanimity.

Jude Bijou, M.A., M.F.T., is a respected psychotherapist, educator, and workshop leader. Her theory of Attitude Reconstruction® evolved over the course of more than 30 years working with clients as a licensed marriage and family therapist, and is the subject of her award-winning book, Attitude Reconstruction: A Blueprint for Building a Better Life.

www.attitudereconstruction.com

AUTHENTICITY

We are constantly invited to be who we are.

– Henry David Thoreau

CHAPTER 2

IF IT COMES FROM THE HEART IT GOES TO THE HEART

BY ED GAELICK, CLU, ChFC

Early in my insurance career, I attended insurance conferences as often as I could. It was motivating to hear some of the best of the best tell their stories of how they became so successful. I could use all the advice I could get. Fortunately, at one of my first conferences, the main platform speaker was an immigrant who came to this country and became one of my industry's top producers. During his presentation, he said something in his native language first and then translated it into English. That statement was one of the most profound statements I have ever heard, a statement that has stuck with me ever since and the one I credit for molding the way I have interacted with my prospects and clients since.

That statement greatly influenced my career and proved to be one of the most important lessons of my business life. Translated he said, "If it comes from the heart, it goes to the heart."

The insurance industry is quantitative and sales-results oriented. Salespeople are taught selling skills and how to overcome objections.

There are sales conferences, countless books on selling, contests, qualification for trips, awards, and plenty of accolades to be given. There is enormous pressure to sell as agencies and insurance companies invest a lot of money to train someone, and they need to recapture their acquisition cost and make money on every investment.

While I understood this is necessary in business, in my view, that shifts the focus from helping the client to qualifying for a trip. I always had a difficult time with that.

What is it that makes some salespeople stand out and excel? Is it superior sales skills or something intangible such as interpersonal skills?

I was always lousy with the selling process but I am really good at focusing on my clients and listening.

I try hard to make sure the people with whom I work know I understand them. I am locked into them, what they are saying, what they are not saying, and their body language. And when I speak, I speak from the heart, and it goes to the heart.

There will always be someone smarter than you. Someone who wakes up earlier, works harder and longer, or sells more than you. What I am convinced has made me stand out in my career is that no one cares more than me, no one. When I speak, people know immediately that I am trustworthy, honest, have morals, and that I care.

The most frequent comment I hear from my clients is, "I trust you." I don't think of sales contests. I have learned that when your intentions are less than pure, when you have commission breath, the prospect will know.

This year I am celebrating my 30th year in the insurance business. Statistics show most life and health brokers and agents find other careers within three years. So why did I last?

Being motivated, working long hours, working smart, providing remarkable service, making a promise and delivering more, constantly learning, doing the right thing, staying healthy, and surrounding myself with excellent people all helped.

Yet with all these things, I believe I would have failed if I didn't care as much, and if I didn't follow "when it comes from the heart, it goes to the heart." Anyone can work hard, work long hours, and know their stuff. But factor in caring, empathy, and understanding, and that is a tough combination to beat. Achieving successful results helping others motivates me, not money. Money comes if you do the right things.

I truly believe one's reputation is the most valuable asset. Once that is lost, it can never be regained.

Bottom line is never do the wrong thing. If it's questionable, don't do it. Get smarter and more creative and figure out ways to do things without compromising integrity.

Not everyone can be a great salesperson but I found a natural way to distinguish myself from many others. I am most comfortable saying selling is a weakness of mine. But I am equally as comfortable saying no one is more connected.

While the story I shared refers to selling, the concept of, "if it comes from the heart it goes to the heart," applies to everything in life.

Ed Gaelick, CLU, ChFC, established PSI Consultants, LLC, in 1985, where he specializes in company-sponsored employee benefits, business planning and personal insurance. Throughout his career, Ed has received many of the highest professional honors awarded in the insurance industry. His dedication, integrity, and fortitude have earned him great respect from his clients, staff, and peers.

www.psi-consultants.com

ABUNDANCE

Some people succeed because they
are destined to, but most people succeed
because they are determined to.

– Unknown

CHAPTER 3

MASTERING BEING THE BOSS OF YOUR INCOME AND YOUR LIFE

BY RENEE GAMBINO

What do success and abundance mean to you? Do they mean giving, sharing, investing, doing, or having? Or do they mean selfish, pretentious, evil or unobtainable? Go back and read those two sentences and be curious how words can describe one thing so differently and impact our world so deeply.

My father didn't ask people, "What's going on?" he used to say, "What's the story?" I never thought about it until I was much older, but asking, "what's the story" makes so much more sense. Whatever we perceive as "what's going on in life" is our own story. And we all have one.

My story started with being born with a last name that was associated with murder, extortion, and gambling. So proud. So what's the story around that? When I took a really good look at my father's top five success strategies, I discovered an amazing paradigm shift in my thinking. I thought, at one time, that all of these teachings were selfish, pretentious, evil, and unobtainable.

Ron Gambino's Top Five Success Strategies

1. "You're a Gambino! That means something!
2. "Don't ever take sh*t from anyone!"
3. "Do it right, or don't do it at all!"
4. "Honey Bunch, I can move mountains!"
5. "If you hurt my daughter, all I have to do is make one phone call!"

What I discovered was the truth in creating a successful business, career, and life.

STRATEGY #1: AWARENESS

"You're a Gambino, and that means something!" Who you were born to be compared to who you are being at all times is what sets you up for success or failure! Resisting who we really are causes internal conflict. (Boy, do I know this!) This shows up in mediocre results in business, relationships, financial freedom, and overall well-being.

Who are you being when you're not getting amazing results in your business, career, and life? Who are you being when you're getting the results you truly want? How can you make that shift much more often?

STRATEGY #2: CONFIDENCE

"Don't ever take sh*t from anyone!" Taking a stand for what you really want can only become a reality if you choose to own your brilliance and your value. Knowing that we are all directly in the path of abundance reminds us that no one is special and we're all meant to receive love, money, spirit, and growth.

What do you stand for? What's non-negotiable for you? How can you bring this deeper into your success path? What do you need to stop tolerating to align with these values?

STRAGEGY #3: ACTIONABLE GOALS

"If you can't do it right, don't do it at all!" I hated when he said this. I felt not good enough and overcompensated by working my ass off striving to be "perfect," which is impossible, of course, and therefore the lowest form of a goal! So what's the story with this?

The diamond here is about doing. Putting your burning desire into actions that lead you always closer to your goal. Mediocre actions equal mediocre results.

Challenging your personal best means increasing the odds for amazing results. All my father was really asking me to do was challenge myself and have the will to win. Of course, I wish I figured that out before I almost killed myself with overworking and undervaluing myself.

STRATEGY #4: BELIEF

"Honey Bunch, I can move mountains!" My father didn't care what anyone thought! This caused limitless moments of embarrassment and fear. But there was so much more to him. How do I know this for sure? When he was 44 he was diagnosed with lymphoma. They told him he'd never see his 50th birthday. He died at 59. He didn't care what the doctors thought. He was in charge. He didn't care what cancer thought. He believed in the power of himself more than the power of proven statistics. He knew to live he had to come before anything else. He, in turn, moved mountains.

When we turn to self, we turn to God, Spirit, Universe or whatever you personally call it. This is when we understand the depth of our true power. We can then eliminate the circumstances that hold us back. We move from a place of authenticity and strength even in the presence of fear and doubt. Belief kicks fear and doubt's ass every time! Guaranteed!

Whose voice do you hear or what tape runs through your mind when you think of having more and reaching your full potential? Safety, security, shame, doubt, fear, don't go too far, what will people think, am I good enough, other people deserve it more than me, other people come first, it's not fair to have more, other people…

If your success were guaranteed, what would you do? Who would you be? How big would you play? Don't move forward without answering these questions. These are the diamonds. This is where your big success is hiding!

STRATEGY #5: SUPPORT AND ACCOUNTABILITY

"If you hurt my daughter, all I have to do is make one phone call!" (My husband remembers this phone conversation with my dad like it was yesterday! Dad made sure the 2500-mile distance meant nothing.) The point is, my father had my back! It was an approach that not everyone understands, but nonetheless, it made me less fearful of the big bad world. Point being, when fear is extinguished, nothing can stop you!

What would change for you if your fear of big success were extinguished? Who's your backup? Who's going to tell you to pull up your bootstraps and give you winning strategies? And if you fall, who will say, "No whining, get up and do it again only smarter this time." With love make your list. These people are important in your journey.

Asking people in your life to support your dreams when they're choosing to suffer from self-doubt and lack-mindedness is setting you up for disappointment. Expecting them to support you just because they love you is asking them to step out of their comfort zone. They have their own story! Just because you're rewriting yours, doesn't mean they'll stop valuing safety and comfort. Stop asking them!

The key is to reach out to people who aren't afraid of you being successful. Who's going to gift you with clarity and the truth? Seek them out. Show gratitude, even if it hurts!

It's a new thought for most, but if there was no other person or thing to blame, what would change for you? Here's the diamond: what changes is, we discover we have total control of our outcomes! Yeah, that means we can be as successful as we could ever dream! Unless you'd rather stand in your own way, of course! Read this paragraph again, because it will seriously change your entire life if implemented.

If you were in full control of your outcomes, what would you do consistently and persistently to have what you desire and deserve? When will you start? Write it down.

I support clients every day to find the truth in their story. To feel the power of their innate gifts. What are your innate gifts? No one is looking. Write them down. I'll bet there's more money and more life for you in there!

For many years I thought my unfiltered way of speaking was unsophisticated. I thought my ability to pinpoint blocks and turn a complicated situation into simple steps was no big deal. It just came natural to me. Wrong! Entrepreneurs and executives love and crave clarity, truth, and strategy.

For many years, I didn't see the magnitude of possibility. The truth is, when we desire more life, we are fully aligned with our natural state. We are born naked, confident, and not afraid to demand what we want and need! God and Universe are just waiting for you to step into your full self-expression and demand a beautiful abundant life! For everyone! Who else would benefit from you having more money and more life?

My dad was a Gambino through and through. He was also a drummer, charismatic, loved to laugh, brave, a great dancer, and loved me deeply in his way. He didn't involve himself in anything that would put his family in serious harms way. Let it be known, you wouldn't have found a shovel in his trunk and no he didn't move to Arizona because he was in the witness protection program! True story!

The steps and strategies my father shared with me came in the form of a not so soft approach. I could complain. I could resist and contract. I could wish he had been gentler with his words. Or I could pull up my bootstraps, not take sh*t from anyone, not care what anyone thinks, be aware of who I am, play bigger, be confident, believe, take responsibility, get support, live in my truth, and be wildly successful, just like I was born to be. Just like my dad taught me. In his way. Like a Boss.

Renee Gambino is an income breakthrough strategist who helps business owners and professionals take their income and life to new levels.

www.ReneeGambino.com

BALANCE

Find joy in everything you choose to do.
Every job, relationship, home ... it's your
responsibility to love it or change it.

– Chuck Palaniuk

CHAPTER 4

FINDING WORK-LIFE SATISFACTION
(HINT: IT'S ALL ABOUT THE BALANCE)

BY HEIDI B. RAVIS, Ed.M., LMHC

As a career counselor and consultant, one of my chief tasks is to help clients find work that is satisfying to them. I guide them through the process of identifying interests, strengths and values in order to gain clues that can lead us to potential fields, roles, and settings that align with those elements. I also help them develop a job search strategy tailored to their specific needs and goals.

For many individuals, a crucial component of career satisfaction is work-life balance. This value often becomes more salient as they adjust to parenthood and the many changes it brings to their lives. With children in the picture, work may become a juggling act, even in two-parent households. Parents may find that a previously satisfying and stable career becomes unmanageable and perhaps even undesirable as they struggle to find time and energy for work, family, and other commitments.

Yet even for those whose children are more independent, or those without children, work-life balance may be a strong priority. By way of illustration, I offer my situation: I left my full-time job after the birth of my second child, and soon began very part-time private practice work. As the children got older and I had more time, I added consulting work to my repertoire, gradually increasing my hours and level of involvement. Now that I am an empty-nester, I am able to take on additional responsibilities and projects. I work from a home office, with no formal schedule. I have the time flexibility to spend time with family and friends, and to pursue my many non-work interests. And when I have the pleasure of pursuing my interests with gusto, I find that I have more energy and enthusiasm for my work.

While the arrangement I have constructed works for me, it may not be possible or desirable for others. Mine is just one example of a lifestyle-friendly career.

In the career exploration process, individuals with many interests and talents often find it difficult to commit to one specific career. If the interests and talents are in seemingly disparate areas (e.g., technical and creative), these individuals may feel that they must find a career that involves all of them or else "give up" something vitally important. This is, understandably, a source of anxiety and confusion.

For a multi-faceted person (and I imagine this describes most of us), there is no one job or career path that will satisfy every interest, skill and value – at least not that I've ever encountered. The challenge is to choose the best fit (or a good fit; there may be no one best fit) and find other outlets for pursuing those additional interests.

These other areas are often central to an individual's life satisfaction and identity. Lack of time and energy to pursue them because of job demands may lead to a decrease in career and life satisfaction and an increase in stress levels.

Significant life events (e.g., parenthood, illness, mid-life, industry changes) sometimes lead to a shift in work values.

At these key transition points, some find that they no longer want to work in their previous fields, but prefer instead to explore new options.

Entering a new phase of life may cause them to reexamine their professional goals. Individuals who previously worked in fast-paced, stressful corporate careers may decide to shift into other fields that provide less income but more intrinsic rewards.

They may choose to utilize skills gained from volunteer work or community involvement. They may opt for part-time or project work rather than full-time employment in order to maintain a comfortable balance.

Parents often seek options that are compatible with their children's school schedules. An example is a nurse who transitioned from a hospital setting to a school setting. Being a school nurse in a nearby district allowed her to synchronize her vacations and hours with her children's. She also found that the school was a less emotionally draining setting for her, which gave her more time and energy for her children and non-work interests.

For some, time flexibility is essential to life-work balance. There are a number of options that lend themselves well to flexible time schedules: freelancing, project-based work, private practice, home-based businesses, to name a few.

If flexible employment is not feasible or preferable, telecommuting may be an attractive option. With advances in technology, many employers now permit – or even encourage – employees to work from home on a full- or part-time basis.

If you have a positive track record at your company, you may want to propose a work-from-home arrangement. It may also be possible to consolidate work hours into fewer days, leaving the other days to pursue outside interests or manage other tasks.

Even if any of the above-mentioned options are not possible or desirable, there are still ways to maintain some degree of balance. Some suggestions:

• Schedule periodic "date nights" with your significant other (even if you're just watching Netflix and eating popcorn after the kids go to sleep). Similarly, find time to get together with valued friends and family members whose company you enjoy.

• When you're at work, focus on work; when you're at home, focus on home. You're likely to feel more productive if you are truly present and "in the moment" in each environment.

• Even if you don't have time to pursue all your interests, be sure to make time for at least some of them: at lunchtime, in the evening, on weekends. Read, write, paint, play sports, work out, meditate, listen to music – even spending a short time on an engrossing and satisfying activity can help restore some modicum of balance.

• Keep an open mind and follow up on intriguing opportunities that present themselves. You may find a solution, or a new pursuit, that you hadn't considered before.

Not everyone has the same options or preferences. A situation which suits one person to a tee might not be the right fit for everyone. As a career counselor, I strive to help my clients find the solution that best fit them.

My observation, though, is that we are all multi-faceted individuals, with interests that transcend work roles and settings. Finding time and space to explore and enjoy those various pursuits often involves a balancing act. The challenge is to develop the optimal balance for one's own satisfaction.

Heidi Ravis, Ed.M., LMHC, Team Leader - Global Services and Domestic and International Consultant for REA, provides career and acclimation services to spouses of relocated employees, and supervises other consultants. She also maintains a private career counseling practice. Heidi is a New York State Licensed Mental Health Counselor and National Certified Counselor.

BREAKING FREE

Leap and the net will appear.

– John Burroughs

CHAPTER 5

THE COFFIN

BY TRACE LEVINSON

The date is December 10, 2013. I sit atop the mountain peaks of Machu Picchu, a staggering 8,000 feet above sea level. The Peruvian hills are untarnished and silent, with the exception of a passing breeze or llama feeding off the green mountainside. For three hours, I remain almost motionless, overwhelmed by the first uninterrupted serenity I have experienced in so many years. A sudden need to carry this sense of peace back into life's overcrowded forefront consumes me. It is time to make a change.

Allow me to back up. At this point, I am 20 years old, a third-year undergraduate rounding out a wonderful semester abroad in Chile with a backpacking trip across South America. I have come up from a loving, supportive family and managed to enroll in one of the country's top universities. The future looks bright. So, what's the problem?

Since I can remember, the expectation to "achieve greatness" has seeped like a thick fog into the back of my mind. I tested well, was told I was gifted and thrust myself into the "advanced track" in elementary school.

When high school came around, life hit hard and fast. Take those 12 honors classes! Become tennis captain and president of the Cool Club! And don't forget that colleges want to see 100+ hours of volunteer work! I checked every possible box to maximize my odds of getting into a top university. And it worked. After a post-Stanford-rejection-self-pity-filled three months, I got into UC Berkeley. Whew! I had made few enough errors to earn my keep in the university lottery.

So off I went, bouldering full speed ahead into the indecipherable future. As I adjusted to university rigor, Cal amplified any and all approval-seeking behavior one hundred times over. Not only was the work harder; my classmates now consisted of 30,000 other students with just as much motivation, self-direction and (often cutthroat) drive toward success as myself. High school's heavy-lifting competition of extracurriculars and APs became college's top-tier internship at that one investment bank or tech startup everyone was talking about. You scored interviews with Facebook and Sachs? You must hold the most irrefutably brilliant mind in the west!

Faint signs of losing myself became clear as I changed majors four times in two years. I would stay up nights scrolling through post-graduate salaries by field of study. When a friend pointed me toward computer science, my hungry freshman mind reveled in the cash that software engineers made out of college.

I, with the help of some equally well-intentioned and misguided peers, convinced myself that a $90,000 starting salary would deem me worthy of the Chosen Ones and Made Its of society. Who cared if I hardly enjoyed or knew anything of the field, not to speak of an ego-shattering summer internship following my first year?

My final decision to "stoop" from Computer Science to Economics (a field I've loved since high school) was near impossible. To offset this act of weakness, I decided to be the very best Economics student at Berkeley. I would get the highest-paying job on Wall Street and show those code-breathing software bastards just how successful a lowly Econ major could be. During my final week abroad in Chile, I applied to every top investment bank I could get my hands on, my ambition to score a prestigious summer internship as booming as it had ever been. Then I left for Peru.

To summarize a clichéd existential crisis, that afternoon in Machu Picchu unleashed a hurricane of inner qualms with my decisions to date. A long-repressed realization hit me like a sledgehammer. I had spent the last decade making externally driven choices in the hopes of gaining others' approval. But, whose? I had, throughout the years, heard stories from peers whose parents ceaselessly drove their expectations and demands of their children through the wall.

I witnessed a few of these poor teens melt into the crash-and-burners of our generation, burdened by the abrupt onset of college independence and an inability to self-motivate. But that was not my case. From sixth grade on, neither of my parents knew more of my grades and activities than I cared to share. They were wonderful, unconditional cheerleaders who, if anything, did their best to protect me from my own self-loathing tendencies. Try getting a B this semester; it will do wonders for you! Their efforts rendered to no avail, even today. If acceptance of failure were a class in school, it would have been the sole F on my report card.

So, the question remains. If not made explicit by those around us, from where does this powerful need for success arise? There seems no clear answer; the invisible cackling hand of society, perhaps.

But in the days, weeks, and months following my return from South America, something new had undeniably awakened in me. A vivid, haunting analogy began to solidify: I had been trapped in a coffin almost my whole life.

During the many thoughtless years moving one foot in front of the other, I imagined myself asleep in that coffin. I was largely unaware of the confinements I placed around myself, subconsciously disregarding true passions for fear of being perceived as lesser than. Be the best. Don't you damn dare fail.

That trip to Peru woke me up. It suddenly became crucial to reevaluate my motives for each action going forward, to think consciously and presently about what I wanted for the future, dropping all acquired notions of success. What a concept! At the risk of beating the metaphor into the ground, this crucial yet excruciating step meant breaking the coffin open and never looking back.

Breaking free is no easy task. Our surroundings hold daunting power over our daily lives, trickling stealthily from what to wear and eat down to the core levels of our beings: which goals to chase or stray from, which lifestyles are respectable or unworthy of fighting for. Is maintaining some structure fundamental to the functioning of society? Sure. But we have work to do in unveiling the façade that there exists one universal set of Atta-Boy decisions that trumps all others. Every individual has tremendous and unique abilities that cannot be ignored. Pursuit of fulfillment is simply futile without them. This reality continues to reveal itself in my life more deeply every day.

So, how do you do it? Where is the elegant formula for overcoming insecurities and going out on a limb for your own piece of greatness?

My own experience has unraveled one powerful clue. The transition must begin by venturing outside of your comfort zone and into the unknown. This has included a whole lot of traveling in my case.

Witnessing cultures that (shockingly!) function without constant judgment of others' choices has been eye opening in ways I could never have predicted. Southeast Asia stands out for me in this respect. If unable to get to another country, uproot yourself even a few cities over. It may not require an indefinite relocation, but certainly more than a week's vacation – enough time to discover some cultural differences that will tweak your own mindset.

Join a new group, one that twists your eyebrows up in discomfort just thinking about it. New is the key. Restricting ourselves to unchanged surroundings and expecting to encounter newfound inspiration is precisely the definition of insanity. The farther you teeter away from all current beliefs and understandings, the more you are guaranteed to learn about others, and about yourself.

After ignoring the wonderfully prestigious internship interview requests, I threw out the investment-banking dream and proceeded to backpack in Asia for the duration of last summer. They were two of the best months of my life. I came back even further motivated to hit the ground running with an authentic self. Today, I am moving toward my passion for a research-driven career, albeit a potentially less lucrative, Atta-Boy choice than my former Wall Street ambitions. It feels real, unforced, and fantastic.

As a very wise friend once advised me, "Leap, and the net shall appear." The right choices, especially the truly pivotal ones, are almost never set out in front of us. It is up to each of us to pursue the paths that keep us ecstatic to wake up each morning and trust that the rest will fall into place. It will, not due to divine intervention or serendipity, but because we have the power to make our own luck by achieving extraordinary feats in the pursuit of true passion. Trust me when I say that when that coffin finally begins to break open, there is no way in hell you will want to step back inside.

Trace Levinson graduated from University of California, Berkeley, with a B.A. in Economics and a minor in Spanish linguistics. He is bilingual, traveling to over 45 countries by the age of 21; he has consistently been a philanthropic activist. He now conducts monetary policy research as an Economic Research Assistant at the Federal Reserve Board in Washington, D.C.

CAREER

Choose a job you love, and you will never have to work a day in your life.
– Confucius

CHAPTER 6

IS IT TIME FOR A CHANGE?

BY JENNIFER WEGGMAN, M.A.

There have been times in my professional career that I did not know what I was going to do next. What had been working was somehow no longer working and I knew I needed to make a change. The power of reflection has led me to uncover some universal truths that are common to many people and their experiences.

Even though we feel that we are the only ones going through something, chances are that others have also experienced the emptiness, confusion, lack of direction, and feeling stuck that being in a job or perhaps career that you have outgrown can bring.

At times people realize, often after much effort and preparation, that they never even wanted to be in their current job except that other significant people in their life encouraged or insisted on that path of action.

So, how do recognize that you are ripe for a career or job transformation? Here are several warning symptoms that may appear:

NO MOTIVATION

There is dread that you have to go be an active participant in a role that you no longer enjoy or even hate. Sunday nights and Mondays can be brutal to go through and often you toy with the idea of calling in sick. Numbing out with excessive addictive behavior may happen.

RELATIONSHIP DETERIORATION

When you are not enjoying how you spend the greater part of your waking hours, you will find that outlets in other areas of your life seem to be going wrong, too. A spouse or partner may begin to irritate or annoy you, you have very little patience with your children, and friendships dwindle as you never feel like participating in or initiating activities that you used to enjoy. You also have co-worker issues that crop up.

OVERWHELMED

Thought of making a change paralyzes you, you are in fear of being laid off/ downsized, and there never seems to be time to focus on a plan of action since you don't even know what you want. You just know it is not this place you find yourself in right now.

PHYSICAL MANIFESTATIONS OF DIS-EASE

When we ignore the situation or "suck it up" and muddle through, often the toll this takes produces illness and pain in the physical body.

If any of these are striking a chord with you, you may be in need of a completely new road map. However, this takes courage!

When I initially went to college, I wanted to be an airline pilot. In my senior year of high school and freshman year of college, I took private pilot lessons and was enrolled in an aviation program at a midwest public university.

As it was the early 1980s, I came to figure out that to get the required number of hours to gain a commercial pilot license would require joining the Air Force and committing to a six-year stint. The Tailhook scandal was coming to light and in addition, the idea of being in an organization that dropped bombs was not very appealing.

My ultimate goal was to be the Rolling Stones private pilot, not have 300 people behind my seat that I had to be responsbile for in a commericial airline situation. The other topper was that women were not yet allowed to be pilots in the Air Force. These aviatrix trailblazers would come a few years later. With all these barriers and obstacles, I had to regroup... and fast!

Taking many prerequisite courses before even getting to the aviation courses, I took many Geography courses like Meterology and Cultural

Geography and enjoyed them very much. I learned there was a Tourism program and I decided to go for that major instead. My underlying belief was that people are the same all over the world.

By encouraging travel, promoting and marketing destinations I could help achieve world peace as everyone would have the opportunity to learn that we really are just human beings even if we look, dress, or talk different.

This vision inspired me! By adapting and going towards what I enjoyed about the courses I was taking, and being open to new possibilities and opportuities, I switched majors and successfully completed my degree.

I went on to gain employment in a governent destination marketing office in the USA for a Canadian province that worked with US travel wholesalers to increase business to locations within the province. It was fun, I got to meet lots of people and, of course, travel. I doubled my salary in six years - I looked forward to going to work!

Looking back on this time, I had no career transformation, road map, coach. I never even asked people to help me consider my options.

By going towards the energy that was positive and enjoyable, I landed in a worthwhile and successful career that I enjoyed for over a dozen years.

It seemed easy to make these major life and career path choices now in hindsight, but it happened gradually over a period of time. My belief is that the universe will line up the resources, information, people, and opportunities for you when you are clear on what you want.

Most of us know what we don't want. And we love to vent and complain, meanwhile often doing nothing to change our situation. From having an occasional bad day at work to the extreme of becoming the negative Nelly or Ned where people actively seek to avoid you, you can recognize with minimal self-awareness that you need to figure out what you do want to do so you can make a plan of action.

When you are young, you can make life and career changes more easily as you have probably not accepted responsibility for a mortgage, car, or raising a family. It is a great time to explore your options and get clear on a path during and beyond college that will be satisfying and fulfilling. Getting to know your values and what is important to you is an extremely valuable exercise.

Working with clients as a career coach now, I ask several powerful questions at the beginning of our collaboration together.

• What do you want?

• What do you need to learn to do that?

• What is getting in your way of getting what you want?

• What would you do if you were not afraid?

In assessing how the client answers these questions, we form a customized *30 Day Road Map* to partner on creative solutions to problems, opportunities, or ideas that come to light from their answers.

While it can be a different scenario for everyone, I see that if they are reaching out to me for career coaching, they are usually beyond wanting to stay stuck and need an objective facilitator and resource to help them design strategies and come up with and execute on a plan of action.

While family and friends may be well meaning, they are not professionally trained coaches who specialize in creative problem solving in a specific area. Often they secretly want you to stay stuck, because they are not seeing you as you could BE, just who you are which is familiar and "safe."

By achieving goals and moving forward, you magnify their inaction in their own life, which makes them uncomfortable. Their fear of change and the status quo may spill over into their "advice."

Let it go if the relationship is no longer serving you, as you are the only one that is going to live your life. Having a confidential and impartial coach in your corner so you can achieve results faster can be well worth the investment in your career and future income.

Now ask yourself this powerful question: How much does staying stuck cost you?

Another career transformation experience that I had more recently was when I left an IT company to go back to school and start my own business.

Due to all the repetitive clicking I was doing, I had a terrible pain in my elbow and wrist due to the volume of spreadsheets and billing invoices. It got so bad that I had to learn to use my left hand. At that point in my life, I had recently been divorced, and was trying to move up in my career at the company, but there was little room for advancement.

I was in major paralyzing fear, knowing that I needed health insurance and a regular paycheck, and while my body was physically breaking down, I had the additional stress of having to decide that I needed to make a career change as my arm could no longer support my job endeavors. I felt like I was ready to jump off the high wire on a trapeze not knowing if I would be caught on the other side.

After making it through three rounds of yearly layoffs, I went forward with a plan to go back to school and quit my job. On my lunch breaks in the years prior to quitting, I took long distance coaching classes and webinars and attended weekend and evening trainings and conferences.

At one point I just realized that the arm pain and knowing that I had outgrown the work I was doing were keeping me up at night and they certainly weren't paying me enough for 24/7 coverage.

That is when I got energized and focused on what next steps I could do to make a career change. The universe was sending me big messages; it just took me a while because I was stuck in fear.

After six months to take action steps on my new road map plan, I left cube nation and have been self-employed as a career and business success coach. The day I turned in my work badge and my resignation letter was a life highlight for sure!

Do not let the fear of the unknown stop you from living today. Make the decision to step back and look at your life and career from 50,000 feet. Hire a professional coach to come along on the journey with you and hold you accountable for creating a customized plan of action and taking steps to follow through on it.

Author and professional coach, Jennifer Weggeman, M.A., provides accountability, support, and structure for individuals, groups, and teams ready for creative opportunities and taking action. Educator of creative problem solving ideas, speaker and facilitator, clients are supported unconditionally to explore, discover, creatively communicate, and package their extraordinary talents, gifts, and expertise.

www.EdgeOfYourGreatness.com

CHALLENGES

Do not let what you cannot do
interfere with what you can do.
– John Wooden

CHAPTER 7

CHALLENGES + OBSTACLES = CHANGE

BY LACI GREER

Have you ever been driving and noticed something in the road that was in your way or caught you off guard? When you are on the road to achieving goals, trying something new, or just minding your own business, obstacles and challenges will occur. And until you make up your mind that obstacles and challenges are bound to happen, there is no way to make it past them to reach your goals.

There was a point in my life when I learned that I had to accept that there were going to be things that tried to stop me when I had a goal in mind. My first big challenge came when I was working and going to school and decided that I needed a change. So I decided to join the military.

When I started the process to join, I was told I had some medical issues. I immediately became frustrated and thought to myself, "What am I going to do now?" I hadn't dealt with things like this before and didn't know that obstacles and challenges could occur. It was then after talking to my mom that I realized that I had to change how I looked at the situation.

After facing this challenge, I proceeded on to basic training where I had no idea what awaited me. I just knew that it was going to be a piece of cake, but boy was I wrong.

Just like a natural disaster, it's nearly impossible to prepare yourself before obstacles can occur, but you can do something about how you handle them when they do. The bottom line is everyone will experience obstacles in his or her life. They can occur on your job or in your daily life. One thing that I believe is everything happens for a reason, but I also know that while you are in the middle of a problem, that it can be difficult to stay positive or see the end result where things work themselves out.

But if you can make it past that initial shock when obstacles occur, you can make it to the end. There is nothing like going through something and coming out on top when it's all said and done.

I remember after graduating from my tech school and relocating to Washington State, I had several obstacles come my way. And instead of getting down on myself when they occurred, I found another route to take. This is one way to look at your situation when obstacles and challenges get in your way. First realize that with challenges come obstacles. And then know that obstacles give you the opportunity to change your mind set in order to change your situation.

Here is the 411. There is nothing we can do to prevent things from going wrong. But if you're able to change your mind set about your challenges and obstacles, then you can change your life.

Obstacles and challenges are just a setup and are strategically placed in your way to detour you to the right destination. When you are faced with a challenge and/or obstacle, do yourself a favor and look your obstacles straight in the eye and tell yourself, "You will not get the best of me and I will make it past this!"

Laci Greer was born and raised in Fort Worth, TX. Laci has been published in Who's Who Poetry Book *four times. Laci works as a computer technician, mentor, and innovator. She is also the founder of MOTIVS, (Motivating Others to Inspire Versus Settling) that offers consulting and freelancing writing services.*

www.lacigreer.com

CHANGE

Change the way you look at things
and the things you look at change.
– Wayne Dyer

CHAPTER 8

UNTIL SOMETHING CHANGES... NOTHING WILL CHANGE

BY JOAN HERRMANN

"You're fat!" "You're stupid!" "You don't have the right education!" "You'll never be able to get the promotion!" "No man will ever want you!" "You're old!" "She doesn't like you!" "You're ugly!" "You can't do anything right!"

Do any of these words sound familiar? While most people would never consider speaking to another with such negative, degrading words, we have no problem saying these things to ourselves. The rant of self-abusive language runs rampant for most on any given day.

It is estimated that the average person has approximately 60,000 thoughts per day, 85 percent of which are negative, and 90 percent of those thoughts are the same thoughts from the day before. Imagine 51,000 negative thoughts running through your mind every day of every week, of every month, of every year – year after year! It's no wonder we feel beaten up, insecure, fearful, and anxious. No one could survive that abuse unscathed.

You've heard the expression, "You are what you eat." Well, just as important, "You are what you think." Your thoughts influence your outlook on life, your attitude toward yourself, and they have a profound impact on your physical and emotional health.

Many people spend a great deal of time complaining about their lot in life: their horrible marriage; their disrespectful children; their bleak financial situation; their dead end, life-draining job. They go on ad nauseum talking about all the reasons why they are miserable.

What they don't realize is that they are creating their reality!

The thoughts that you have day after day cause you to make the same choices day after day. These same choices generate the same behavior. The same behavior provides the same experiences. The same experiences create the same emotions. And the same emotions spark the same thoughts.

If you're one of those people who is thinking the same thoughts day in and day out, complaining, feeding the loop, how will tomorrow be different from today?

Albert Einstein defined insanity as doing the same thing over and over again and expecting a different result. Sound familiar?

If it does, odds are that you suffer with a health issue, are depressed or anxious, stressed out, and not living a fulfilled life. You may be constantly looking for something external – a new car, bigger house, money, recognition, fancy clothes, a job promotion – to make you happy. All the time not realizing that happiness and contentment is an inside job. If you need proof of this, just look at the people that experience horrific tragedy or live in poverty, yet they express gratitude and are blissfully happy.

So … where does lasting change begin?

In your head!

What goes on in your head has the power to impact every aspect of your life.

Simply put, every time you have a thought, the brain creates chemicals that are circulated throughout your body. If you have happy, positive thoughts, the brain produces good chemicals that make you feel good and enhance the body. When you have negative thoughts, the brain produces chemicals that make you feel bad and are detrimental to the body. When you feel good or bad, you make thoughts that equal how you feel, which in turn produces those types of chemicals, and so on.

Over time, your way of thinking creates a state in which the mind and body work together. Depending on your thought pattern, this can result in a positive way of life, or dis-ease.

Before you can eliminate negative self-talk, you must recognize that it's happening. Tune in to your way of thinking, pay attention to what's going on inside your head.

Determine what underlying themes or messages are behind your negative thoughts. What were some of the triggers? What activities or people triggered negative thoughts?

Evaluate the validity of the thoughts. Ask yourself if there is any truth to what you're thinking. Are there things you can change? Which thoughts are garbage that must be deleted?

Ask yourself how you can change the negative thought to a positive one. Instead of looking at situations in the worst light, try to find the positive aspects and focus on them. Avoid thinking about the worst-case scenarios. They usually never happen.

Monitor your thoughts. When you are thinking negatively, stop yourself as soon as you realize it and replace the negative thought with your "new thought." Even though negative thoughts will always come up, the perseverance you develop will keep you going and after time the old thoughts will be replaced with the new ones.

We have all experienced things in life that make us want to throw up our arms and shout "uncle!" It's easy to give up, check out, and wallow in misery. But, speaking from experience, that's no way to live. What you do with your life is a choice and you have the power to turn the bleakest situation around. As Henry Ford eloquently stated, "Whether you think you can, or you think you can't, you're right." You have tremendous power within and it's time to tap into it.

Joan Herrmann is the founder of a multimedia communications company and created, hosts, and produces the radio show Change Your Attitude…Change Your Life. Joan also publishes a monthly digital magazine, Change Your Attitude…Change Your Life: 24/seven, *which is distributed to thousands worldwide. Her guest and magazine contributors list reads like a who's who of the most influential and inspirational people in the world. A published author and motivational speaker on the topics of transition and self-empowerment, Joan has been featured in print and broadcast media. Her speaking engagements include the New Jersey Governor's Conference for Women and The Power of Positive Medicine with Dr. Bernie Siegel. Joan offers hope with her message about the power of positive thoughts and intentions, and she guides people on how to embrace and deal with change instead of fearing and hiding from it.*

www.cyacyl.com

COURAGE

Truth is powerful and it prevails.

– Sojourner Truth

CHAPTER 9

THE COURAGE TO TELL THE TRUTH

BY ANN SHEYBANI

I teach writing workshops – locally and online – and I also coach people pleasers who are sick of feeling trapped by their inability to tell the truth; who want to learn how to draw boundaries and say no.

A while back, I recognized an interesting similarity between my two sets of clients. Writers, like people pleasers, often find themselves paralyzed by the fear of telling the truth, of revealing themselves on paper. This fear translates into writers' block and/or boring or confusing prose. I also discovered that memoir writers, in particular, are often the product of dysfunctional families.

Like people pleasers, they were taught from childhood not to reveal their family secrets. They were told, "Don't air dirty laundry." They were discouraged from telling the truth even amongst family members, even to themselves. As you might appreciate, this old rule has a way of mucking up the creative works.

It took me a few years of writing (not to mention therapy) to recognize why my own work continually fell short of the mark. I was writing about people I'd known while living in Iran and their own tragic stories; about culture shock; about my own marriage, frustrated by serious cultural differences and an army of in-laws who regularly ate my liver for dinner.

I wanted to capture the effect that living in Iran had had on me. I wanted to uncover, mostly for myself, how I had ended up so over my head in the first place, and yet my stories lacked depth. They were sarcastic and had no point. They were burdened by a smokescreen of justification. There were big jumps in the timeline and in logic because I had left out important incidents that I was too afraid to reveal.

One day I came across Anne Lamott's book, *Traveling Mercies*. I fell in love with Lamott because she threw a spotlight on all the bad stuff that lurked in my own heart; all the fear I had about myself. And in a book about finding God, about grace and personal salvation, Lamott wrote about the messy life that had led to her transformation.

Though the details were different, I immediately recognized myself: "Life was utterly schizophrenic. I was loved and often seemed cheerful, but fear pulsed inside me. I was broke, clearly a drunk, and also bulimic. One night I went to bed so drunk and stuffed with food that I blacked out....I made seven thousand dollars that year and could not afford therapy or enough cocaine. Then my married man called again, and we took to meeting in X-rated motels with lots of coke, tasteful erotic romps on TV like *The Bitch of the Gestapo....*"

Her writing was, to use her own words, "so sexy and intimate and stark that you almost have to look away." I wanted to lift her words and rearrange them on my page because "Everything is usually so masked or perfumed or disguised in the world, and it's so touching when you get to see something real and human."

It dawned on me, then, that what was missing in my own writing (not to mention life) was honesty. I had started writing with the idea of, "Look what happened to me!!" But what I needed to explore was the deeper question of, "Look, what happened to me?"

I wanted to be real like Lamott. I decided, then, that it was OK to be the flawed hero of my own tale: A damsel in distress who was also manipulative, insecure, aimless, and confused. It wasn't my job to look good; it was my job to write about the glaring mistakes, the failed expectations, and the hearts that got broken; to admit that I wasn't just an innocent victim. I began to recognize things about myself that I hadn't before. I began to understand the role I had played, the choices that I had made, how I had been responsible.

It took me ages to see that, for every sin I've committed, there's someone else out there who carries the same sense of shame, and that has spurred me on. That has made me dig deeper in my writing, to say what most people are afraid to say; to say what I'm afraid to say.

I believe that in order to get what we want most in life – connection with others – we have to have the courage to tell the truth, regardless of who will disapprove. We have to allow ourselves to be vulnerable. We have to risk opening ourselves up to criticism.

At the beginning of each writing term, we deal with the biggest fear participants have: the negative reaction of friends and family to their writing. It's this paralytic fear that prevents folks from putting anything down on paper, or from telling it like it is/was, or from pursuing publication when they finish their project.

This fear of disapproval applies to us all, particularly people pleasers. One negative comment, one offended look, and there we go questioning ourselves, our motivation, our value, and our numerous failings. Everything changed in my life when I stopped hiding who I really am/was. The world opened up and I grew to approve of myself, even though I sometimes put others off.

Putting yourself out there is the best exercise there is for standing in your own power. To own your own opinions, your own story, is to set yourself free. But let's be real: there are consequences to writing about yourself and others.

Beyond the usual nastigrams we all receive the second we hit "publish," and the occasional embarrassed look I get when someone's read the rare piece I've done about sex, there have been costs for me. By breaking the family rules, I've pissed people off, or sent them reeling. My mom read something I wrote years ago and got her nose out of joint. She made the decision not to read my work; which freed me up. But, machismo aside, it doesn't make me feel good to know she disapproves.

I write about very adult topics, about my relationship with my children's dead father, and some of the things I've revealed have been far too much for them to take. I believe the revelation that their father took a second wife while he was married to me changed the course of my daughter's life in particular. I wish I could take those words back.

Over the years, I've had a wonderful outpouring of support and love from readers. I learned that what I had to say – as hard as much of it was for me to do so—made a positive difference in their lives. For this reason alone

I will often tell my writing students this: Your REAL audience is desperately waiting for you to put into words what they are feeling, what they are yearning to hear.

None of us can write well worrying about what other people think. We have to tell the truth and deal with it all later. One of the reasons people write memoir or personal essay is to learn about themselves and/or the important people in their lives. It is a journey of discovery. But we must tell the truth.

Write as if no one will ever read your words. That makes for interesting books. If we don't tell the truth, our stories will be dead in the water. Take the pages into the back yard and bury it, right now, because politeness is boring. Listen to me. Courage. Take courage.

It's our job, our privilege, to allow others into our world. There are people out there suffering the wounds and sorrows and terrors of existence who do not have the words to weather it, and it is the writer's place to give expression to that part of experience – to provide a sense of what Joseph Conrad called the "solidarity of the human family," and to give forth nothing less than the knowledge that no one, in the world of stories and of art, is ever totally alone. When we tell our truth, someone out there will read our words and feel hope.

I love what Brené Brown says about telling the truth: "It's crazy how much energy we spend trying to avoid these hard topics when they're really the only ones that can set us free." All along you have carried in your pocket the key to set yourself free. Tell the truth.

EXERCISE

• Take out a clean sheet of paper and a pen

• At the top of the page write this phrase: The last thing I want anybody to find out about me is….

• Set a timer for 10 minutes

• Write whatever comes to mind in response to the prompt above. Don't stop. Don't lift your pen, or hesitate, or worry about spelling or grammar, or your mother.

• This is your dirty little secret. This is what keeps you sick.

Ann Sheybani received her masters in Creative Writing and Literature from Harvard University.

www.annsheybani.com.

DIVORCE

Storms make trees take deeper roots.

– Dolly Parton

CHAPTER 10

A NEW THEORY ON DIVORCE, A BETTER WAY!

BY LINZI LEVINSON

I believe that we are trained to presume that the courts and the legal system, along with the attorneys, are the only options we have for severing a marriage / family unit.

I propose a novel and innovative approach to this devastating process; the standard process infrequently releases involved parties without shackles and scars when utilizing the court system. I propose that you, personally, lead by seeking out a tailored solution for your distinctive situation. No two circumstances are identical, so why walk through a "vanilla" process that is not capable of serving the individual needs of your particular family members?

If you step out of conformity, you have just taken your first step toward freedom.

The goal should be to create a team. The team you would create is one that would provide support and that would prohibit judgment of any kind; this team would be one that would guarantee results intended to meet your very fundamental needs. This team would be dedicated to reduction or the potential elimination of the monumental expenses that the court and legal systems require should you be engaged in divorce.

You should be seeking an approach that is ultimately healthy, affordable, realistic, and relationally holistic. You would be amazed at some of the potential integrative team strategies that are possible. It is imperative that you resolve this divorce process with safety such that you can begin the celebration of your new life.

Life is challenging, and relationships can be very unpredictable. Pain, however is not a necessary way of life, and suffering is unacceptable. The team that you should be constructing could or would include licensed and certified professionals. Lawyers, counselors, coaches, mediators, conflict-resolution specialists, sexuality educators, intimacy consultants, certified relationship specialists, paralegals, and even massage therapists and holistic yoga coaches. These professionals can all serve a tremendous purpose in keeping you and your family members safe, productive, communicative, and healthy.

Additionally, joining support groups that augment "divorce support" is valuable. Groups that work with teen sexuality, LGBT issues, women's empowerment, anger management, single dad dilemmas, children going through divorce, and intimacy in relationships are just a few to contemplate and investigate.

If you're looking for additional support and guidance through a challenging relational situation or you are just ready to take yourself toward the life you know you deserve, facilitating this kind of a crew will activate the methodology that can generate the positive result leading to sustainable wellness.

Sad does not ever have to be "bad," and with every challenging situation, there is always a blessing to be found.

The specialists mentioned prior could offer the option of couples counseling for those who may be on the verge of divorcing; these experts and professionals may even be able to resolve a bond that appeared hopeless. This group of professionals can present a means to dissolving marriage in a tranquil, amicable fashion.

Avoiding the court system can assist in removing restraining orders and help ensure that the fees are kept low, but the objectives of both of the parents can be met. It is possible for everyone to be on the same side. What a concept!

Family counseling can transpire for the whole family and is often extremely beneficial. Co-parenting counseling can and should take place to provide amicable relations for parenting so that the children can remain in healthy homes going forward.

Children are often neglected in this process; ensuring that they have their own dedicated coach, counselor, therapist, or professional to navigate them through the entire journey is essential.

This dedicated attention to the children will greatly intensify and expand their probabilities of recovering and traveling through this upheaval with their self-esteem intact. This will change how the rest of their life goes. It matters.

The mission of creating an alternative divorce strategy is to circumvent the expensive attorney costs associated with the fast-growing population of couples who find they are confronting the overwhelming expense linked directly to the decision to dissolve their marriage.

In some cases it is only one of the parties that want the divorce, while in other cases, it may be both; in either case, the inevitable default route is commonly the process of Family Law Litigation. This launches extensive and ongoing attorney fees.

The divorce rate has now surpassed 50 percent. For second marriages, it has passed 60 percent. For third marriages, the divorce rate is now reporting statistics past 70 percent. With these terribly concerning growth rates, this just reaffirms the urgency to create a system and schema that is focused precisely on contributing to healthier marital victory, and to reinforcing more wellness through what may ultimately be the necessity of a marital dissolution. Attention to this is long overdue.

Family members (especially children) are getting shattered in the aftermath of these grueling divorces attached to these astounding statistics.

The children of divorce are proven to have far less self-esteem than those who come from nuclear families. The results and ramifications in studies of these children after divorce are worth serious reflection.

The amicable ending is critical, although in our society, we are losing site of why it is so crucial to sever relationships with some form of health intact.

If we contemplate these facts, it makes sense that wounds can be more damaging then expected, and will most likely become permanent.

If there are children involved, even in the smoothest of divorce situations, just the longevity of the divorce has a tremendous impact on the child (or children). Many parents do not realize this because they are so immersed in the actual logistics and personal emotions of the divorce. The financial drain of the divorce also has lasting effects on the children; this habitually gets ignored.

Predominantly, when there are the two divorce attorneys, by the mere definition of the process, there have to be two sides. There must then be a winner and a loser. The kids will usually be caught somewhere in the middle.

There are also couples that have divorced, and cannot seem to master co-parenting without generating major pain and suffering for themselves and the children involved. Many of these parents (and step parents) find that only by going back to court can they attempt to solve issues that are complex, or simple.

Complex issues regarding changing schools, and simple issues such as whether to get the child contacts or glasses, braces, go to sports camp, travel out of country, or even just getting a haircut, can often be "taken to court" as the means to get a decision made. This is not only financially draining, but also transports stress directly to the children, keeping them in a state of anxiety and compromised health.

Collaborative Divorce has been introduced as a recent model for amicable dissolution, when this is not a proven model for success, and in fact, may be proving to the contrary.

The cost is not cheaper in that both parties pay their own attorneys, and accumulate expenses due to the fact that they each pay their own coaches. The parties correspondingly pay child coaches (if needed). These attorneys and coaches get together consistently in a "collaborative effort." The bills can quickly add up (and the clients are often not even aware of the growing bills).

The collaborative intention of so many people "getting along" in all of these "feel-good meetings" can ultimately be financially and emotionally draining and stressful. This can cause more arguing, less results, more pointing fingers, with less accountability.

The questions then remains, where is the logic in how Collaborative Divorce provides resolution for the couple such that the cost is kept low, and the dissolution and health of the couple (and children) is preserved. Might this model in actuality just be a cookie-cutter template designed solely for profit?

Each individual and couple must make the choice that is fitted for their specific situation, but we often just default to what society has implemented. It is predictable that we will conform to what already exists.

We often assume that the practice of marital dissolution necessitates that we include the courts, judges, and attorneys; we accept that parties must battle one another. We are taught that there will be a winner and there will be a loser.

We almost always lose sight of the provisions needed for the children. The potential demise of our youth is rarely a topic that we are educated about.

The suffering of our children during this experience is pure torture, and it is our responsibility to get resourceful. We must become leaders who now invent new ways to dissolve marital relations. It is our duty as adults to develop innovative and holistic approaches to sever nuclear family units.

It is our responsibility to ensure that while the "bricks we must carry" through dissolution are likely to be exceptionally burdensome, these bricks are purely for the adults to carry and ultimately dismantle. They are never to be carried by or handed to our children.

Linzi Levinson practices Relationship Counseling/Comprehensive Life Coaching and she hosts two internet radio shows with over 100,000 followers. She has a master's degree in Counseling Psychology and is a certified relationship specialist - American Psychotherapy Association. Linzi is certified in Conflict Resolution/Mediation - Pepperdine Law School.

www.qualityforlifecoaching.com

EMOTIONS

What lies behind us and what lies before us are
tiny matters compared to what lies within us.

– Ralph Waldo Emerson

TRANSFORMING SELF-BETRAYAL IN THE MIRROR OF RELATIONSHIPS –EX'S, ENEMIES AND OTHER EARTHLINGS

BY JULIE GENOVESE

When my hubby, Bill, had told his ex, Ann, that I was pregnant with our first son, she'd said, "That woman should not be passing on her bad genetics to another generation."

Criminy. I'd imagined folks who'd felt that way about my dwarfism, but she was the first broad to blurt it out.

It was 10 years down the line, after their divorce, and Ann was still railing against Bill. She hadn't let their daughter come to our wedding. She'd made visitations difficult. She blamed and badgered.

Occasionally she threw some ridonkulous zingers at me. After I'd gnaw on them awhile, I'd try to let 'em go. As Anne Lamott wrote, "Not forgiving is like drinking rat poison and then waiting for the rat to die." Thankfully, Ann lived across country - I never had to face the rat. Until.

My step daughter was getting married. We'd be flying out west. Ann would have the home-field advantage. Gulp.

Suddenly, the old grudges I'd "let go," were squawking. My fear started rehashing the past; Ann is critical, defensive and needs to be RIGHT. She tells herself she's better than I am. Will she make a scene at the wedding?

What was it about Ann that I was fighting in myself? Where could I find common ground for the sake of my step daughter? It's 10 years down the line and I am still critical, defensive and needing to be RIGHT. I tell myself I'm better than her. Hmm. Rings a bell.

I decided to have regular (imaginary) soul-to-soul conversations with Ann as I go to bed. It would be an ongoing prayer in hopes of bridging our differences. I'd try, for once, to visualize Ann as a friend. A sister. Underneath the hairy heartaches, I believe we're one human family. We're mirrors of each other's unresolved pain. Here was an opportunity to test my mettle.

Bill had told me a bit about Ann's tough childhood. She and I had probably shared similar humiliation and loneliness. Who hadn't? In our soul-to-soul, I told her I understood. That she was lovable, anyway. She was stronger than she thought. I saw her shoulders and defenses drop. Our eyes teared up. In the end, we hugged like sisters. Laughed over our pettiness. And she'd apologize.

The next night, I imagined a conversation with Ann about motherhood. I'd silently criticized her parenting, a LOT. Now that I had my boys, I told her, I could better understand why she'd been a protective mama bear. I could sympathize with the mayhem of single parenthood. I was rooting for her. We ended up hugging and laughing.

Our conversations went on for several weeks. Often, I still regressed into finger pointing over some past insult. It was embarrassing how I'd held onto them, just like her. I'd be sure to end the visualization with us hugging and laughing. And she'd apologize.

As the wedding drew closer, I was feeling . . . better. Whether or not my prayers reached Ann was no longer the point. Whatever happened, I was dropping my old BS (Belief Systems) so I could step back and see her soul. Without the old defenses within me, I could remember the beauty within her.

Our family flew out for the wedding. As we pulled into the parking lot of the venue where we'd be seeing Ann, Bill said in shock, "There she is." Oh no. Ambush.

I tried to shake off the nerves. I slammed the car door and, with determination, I smiled and headed for Ann. But in my intense focus, I somehow missed seeing the tiny curb ahead. I'd built up enough momentum that when my clog caught the lip, suddenly I became a speed-walking projectile, careening straight toward Ann. Oh help.

My replacement hips and knees have little flexibility, so by the time I reached her, I was practically horizontal. As I felt myself going down, panic erupted. But wouldn't you know. Ann . . . caught me. She didn't let me fall - she lifted me up. She straightened what had gone crooked.

The beauty of the metaphor was lost on me. I felt like a clumsy idiot at the feet of my old foe. But somehow, together, we ended up . . . hugging. And laughing. And I apologized.

The weekend went shockingly well. Ann was a kind hostess; she asked if my boys needed snacks; she offered me a quiet place to rock my youngest to sleep; she complimented Bill on his toast to the beautiful bride. Shut the front door.

At the wedding table that day, as we dined on humble pie, I felt a sweet peace being gratefully served up, too. My soul-to-soul talks had soothed their toughest target - me. Who knows if Ann, too, had been praying for help. For healing. For the love of her only daughter. For her past and her ex. For soulful understanding across the great divide.

Life presents us with endless opportunities to heal the undeveloped parts of ourselves in the mirror of our relationships. Here's another example of how our gripes against others are a Mayday call about our own disconnection from our soul's love.

One evening, my hubby, Bill, tells me about a fight between Ky, our 10-year-old, and Carlito, Ky's best friend. Ky told Bill... that Carlito told Ky... that I was ugly.

Bill stops for a split second. I act unfazed, so he continues nonchalantly. Little does he know, an old sad story has scurried out from behind my eyes. My mad attempt to squelch it is about to backfire. On both of us.

While my rational adult-self assumes that Carlito's comment was to get back at Ky (for something Ky did or said) my younger-self, remembering a childhood of insults about my dwarfism, feels a fearful sting. What is so ugly about me? Damn it, I should be over this insecurity!

I wait for Bill to sooth my embarrassing fears... without my having to voice them. But when he doesn't shower me with compliments, kisses, and Krispy Kremes, the smack-down begins. Ugly is no longer the issue. Bill is now on the chopping block.

I tell myself, If Bill doesn't understand my pain, he never will. Shame zips me over to the dark side. I see Bill there. Growing horns. He's stepping into my BS minefield. I've already been blown to smithereens. He's next.

And he's toast. Note how skillfully mental BS can make the argument about something else, entirely. Since inner BS isn't true or kind, it desperately scrambles to be right.

I grab for the old defenses. Blame. Anger. I think these puppies can lessen the hurt by casting the problem off me. I'm judging myself, but I need to prove that Bill is doing it. Ay caramba.

I expect that my hero hubster should see right through my charade and save me. He should recognize what I deny. This never ends well.

With rapid fire, I tell Bill how he should show his love for me (since I'm not doing it) by acknowledging my old wound (ditto on that denial.)

I was guilty of every one of my charges against him. I stopped loving me the moment I judged my feelings as weak and childish. I projected my judgment onto Bill. I didn't recognize my self-betrayal in his mirror.

No problem. When we deny our feelings, it will seem as if our pain is outside us, crawling all over someone else. Like Ann. Or Bill. How convenient.

We can't run from their reflection because, on a soul level, we are One with them.

Bill goes to bed, angry and confused. I hate admitting it – what I claim about him is true about me. Repeat arguments are a festival of Biblical-sized BS. I order up another slice of humble pie and apologize to Bill in the morning.

Like children, our emotions will clamor for the validation and love we've denied them. They'll go viral in the movie all around us - in the characters who criticize us. Call us fat. Say goodbye.

Our emotions are earmarks that our BS is out of synch with our soul, which only sees us with love and acceptance. We're suffering because we choose to believe otherwise. We can uncover the BS about ourselves by looking at where our fingers are pointing. Do we need the advice we hoist on others? Bless the mirror that calls us names?

Beauty is not in the way we look, but in the way we love. When we allow our war-torn fears to come back home, we can romance our humanness back toward the light. We melt into truth each time we honor our broken, flawed wholeness. Our soul remains unshaken by whatever ugliness we barrel into.

When we embrace the mirrors in our life, soul-to-soul, and welcome ourselves with open arms, we become a beautiful sight.

Julie Bond Genovese is an inspirational speaker, creative soul coach, artist and author of award-winning memoir, Nothing Short of Joy. *Being born a dwarf, with degenerative arthritis, wasn't the poison Julie originally believed - it became the cure.*

www.nothingshortofjoy.com

ENERGY

The energy of the mind is the essence of life.

– Aristotle

CHAPTER 12

THE ATTITUDE OF YOUR ENERGY

BY JOSEPH P. GHABI, M.S.

Attitude determines the quality of your energy. The choices you make, either positive or negative, determine your reality. You are where you are today because of the choices and decisions you make every single day.

Adding to that is the choice of the words you speak and think. For example: I am unhappy, unfulfilled, and unsuccessful, or, I am truly thankful and grateful that I am happy, fulfilled, and successful.

Which of those two statements sounds better to you? Each statement will present a different outcome. If you are investing your energy in either statement, which means you are using the same energy either way, then choose wisely.

Every word you choose determines your reality. The choices you make vibrate with their own energy and play tunes with different frequencies.

The more you use these energies in your life, the more you will develop positive or negative feelings. What song are you playing in your life? It's your choice. The beauty here is that each feeling has its own frequency. Those frequencies play key notes on the instrument we call life.

How did life treat you yesterday and is it still treating you the same way today? If you feel lost and wonder how to interpret your energy and the signal you are sending the Universe, the good news is, there is a simple way and you have the power in your own hands!

First, understand that everything is energy. A table has different energy than a sofa or a TV. Even your name and your brother's or sister's names have a different energy, even if you are from the same family.

I have analyzed people's names and realized that by dropping a letter from a name, which represents a frequency from the individual's vibrational energy, their outcome could be changed. What do I mean? Let's take my first name alone as an example:

Every letter converts into a number in Numerology (see table below). Keep adding all numbers until you have 1 digit.

Table

1	2	3	4	5	6	7	8	9
A	B	C	D	E	F	G	H	I
J	K	L	M	N	O	P	Q	R
S	T	U	V	W	X	Y	Z	

My name is Joseph in French = 161578 = 28/10/1.

The particular energy of Joseph is 1 which is represented with 4 different combinations of frequencies- 0, 1, 2 and 8.

My name is Joe in USA = 165 = 12/3.

The particular energy of Joe is 3 which is represented with 3 different combinations of frequencies 1, 2 and 3

My name is Josef in Afrikaans = 16156 = 19/10/1.

The particular energy of Josef is 1 which is represented with 3 different combinations of frequencies 0, 9 and 1.

My name is Youssef in Arabic = 7631156 = 29/11/2.

The particular energy of Yousef is 2 which is represented with 3 different combinations of frequencies 1, 2, 9 and 11.

If I used all of these names in my life, I would be the most confused person you'd know! The more names you use determines the level of confusion you have. The more names you have, the more complex life is for you.

The same goes with the following feelings:
Stress = 129511 = 19/10/1
Successful = 1333511633 = 29/11/2

So let's use the word stress as an example, which equals 19/10/1. If you have the vibration 1, 9, 0 in your core vibration in your chart, when you are on the negative side of these vibrations, you are vulnerable to having more stress in your life. When you are aware of that fact, however, then you can handle your stress more easily.

If you use the Psychosomatic Numerology (Psycho = mind and Somatic = body) and we go back to the word stress, the Vibrations 0 and 9 effect your Brow Chakra. Some of the physical problems relating to the Brow Chakra are tension headaches, migraines, visual defects, short-sightedness, long sightedness, glaucoma, cataracts, catarrh (swelling of the mucous membranes in the head in response to an infection), sinus problems, and even some ear problems.

Vibration 1 affects your Crown Chakra and some of the physical problems relating to the crown chakra are depression, Parkinson's disease; schizophrenia, epilepsy; senile dementia; Alzheimer's, many mental disorders, confusion, dizziness, and feeling as though you have a fuzzy head.

It's easy to see how important it is to have our mind and emotions in harmony and operating on a positive scale. That way we can avoid having any unnecessary disease.

Since everything is energy, when we change the polarity of this energy, there will be a different outcome.

So, technically, you are 100 percent responsible for where you are today in your life and you have the opportunity to completely change your reality.

Changing your attitude will bring you a new energy and new doors will open up for you. Everything is your choice. You have the choice to be angry or at peace. You have the choice to be miserable or happy. You have the choice to be depressed or be successful.

No one is preventing you from being whatever you'd love to be.

Joseph P. Ghabi, M.S., is a numerologist, healer, and spiritual leader who speaks on topics ranging from relationships and the law of attraction to life purpose and past histories. He is known for his expertise in finding your authentic peace with the past. Joseph is a #1 best-selling author of The Blueprint Of Your Soul *and hosts his own radio show.*

www.FreeSpiritCentre.ca

GIVING BACK

We can't help everyone,
but everyone can help someone.
– Ronald Reagan

CHAPTER 13

TRANSFORMATION THROUGH VOLUNTEERISM

BY DEBRA WILBER

Ghandi said, "The best way to find yourself is to lose yourself in the service of others." There are many ways you can be in service of others. Being a volunteer is one; my experience as a volunteer provided the fuel for my transformation.

A few years ago, I found myself retired with lots of time and not a lot to do. What I want to share with you is the role volunteerism played in my transformation from retiree to entrepreneur and how it can be the fuel for yours!

Becoming a volunteer isn't as easy as you think. You could just show up at the next organization looking for volunteers, but the likelihood of success isn't great. You are about to donate one of your most precious resources – your time! Don't make a hasty decision and give it away to any organization looking for help. Use discretion and find a volunteer opportunity that is a good fit for you and your goals. Yes, goals.

As a coach, I help individuals feel confident and ignite their transformation. I use volunteerism as an opportunity to build confidence and try new things. With this in mind, we write goals that focus on volunteer experiences that support our coaching objectives.

While every situation is unique, you can start by answering the question: What do I hope to achieve through volunteering? Start your list with the first thoughts that come to mind then continue your list with the things you like to do, the causes you like to support, and what you enjoy most about your friends. The list will evolve over time with your volunteer experiences.

Based upon my experience, here are five steps to find a rewarding and transforming volunteer experience:

1. Document. Get a small notebook that you can carry with you to serve as your volunteer journal. Your first documentation exercise will be your goals as discussed above. It's doesn't need to be a long list, begin with a few items that are important to you and find a volunteer opportunity that matches. A quick internet search will yield many possible volunteer opportunities.

Once you have volunteered, documenting your experience is important on a number of levels. Always document your time, your expenses, and your mileage. The volunteer journal is an easy solution to document these items, but do whatever works for you and provide this information to your accountant or tax preparer each year and they can determine if it applies to your situation.

More important than the potential tax write-off, document how you feel while you are in the process. Pay attention to your behavior. Are you energized and looking forward to your next volunteer shift? If yes, you might have found your tribe. If not, then it's time to evaluate the experience and consider a new opportunity.

Also, keep track of the new people that you meet. Exchange business cards or write their contact information in your journal. Every person you meet is on purpose and part of your transformation journey. Some will become part of your tribe, some will inspire you, and some will teach you a lesson and move on. It's all part of the process.

2. Find Your Tribe. When you donate your time, select an organization that meets your goals and with people you enjoy. This is not an either/or proposition. Use your list of goals to seek out volunteer organizations that are a match.

Your love and support of the organization will fulfill your goals and fill your heart while bringing you closer to finding your tribe. There are good days and bad days in the life of a volunteer. Finding your tribe will bring you back after the bad ones.

You will be interacting with people: volunteers, the volunteer organization and the people they support. You want to enjoy the time you spend with fellow volunteers. It may take a few volunteer shifts to assess this, but don't diminish the importance of connecting and building relationships with volunteers and the organization. They are part of your new network.

3. Don't Give Up! You may not find your tribe on your first volunteer outing! It's okay. I spent a year as a serial volunteer donating my time to several organizations until I found my tribe. I didn't write goals, I selected volunteer experiences where I had talent to share.

Usually, the organizations recognized me as soon as I arrived: smiling, eager to help, willing to do just about anything. They put me to work and in most cases I returned a second and third time. Eventually, I realized that either the organization or the people weren't a fit for me.

If this happens to you it's okay, thank the organization and continue your search. You didn't fail, you clarified what you want and need in a volunteer experience. Add to your list of goals then continue to search for your tribe.

An easy mistake is to look for a volunteer assignment that can only utilize your talent instead of fulfilling your goals. For example, I love to cook. One of my first volunteer experiences was cooking dinner for a group home. I did very little research into the organization or people. I thought, I can cook, I am a team player, this is going to be great! It wasn't so great for me. The volunteer team was okay, the experience was okay and the recipients of the meal were appreciative. But when I left my shift, I felt drained and not energized. It took me a couple volunteer shifts to realize, this is not my tribe. I wasn't aligned with the organization or the people.

4. Give 'til it hurts but set limits! Once you find your tribe and you are blissfully donating your time and talent to an organization, you might find that it is hard to say no or set limits. Your volunteer tribe needs you, a passionate volunteer, but they also need a volunteer that is not suffering from burn-out or frustration because you do not have work-life-volunteer balance. Balance is important.

When I finally found my tribe, I was there every day. Not once a week or when my schedule allowed, I was there every day because I found my tribe and I loved it. You are in control of your time. Set limits for yourself that work for both you and the volunteer organization.

5. Transform. If you approach volunteerism as an opportunity to give away your time, you will reap what you sow. You will give away your time. But, if you approach volunteerism as an opportunity to serve others and be open to the experience, you will discover an amazing transformation.

When you find your tribe, you find your spark, your purpose! Joy comes back into your life. You smile more. You are happier. You think clearly and make better decisions. You are on your way to transforming yourself through the service of others.

I found my tribe on the fourth volunteer experience in my year of serial volunteerism. I was looking for an opportunity for my retired parents. We signed up together for a local semi-annual rummage sale. We received good volunteer assignments and worked hard throughout the sale.

This experience was different from the beginning. I was familiar with the organization and supported their mission. My volunteer team was a great group of women from all walks of life also aligned with the organization's mission. I quickly realized they were my tribe. The more I volunteered and experienced the positive energy, the more I could feel myself coming back to life. It was like I put on a new pair of glasses and could see things a bit more clearly. During that first sale, I found the coaching program I use today. And within six months I opened my business. Coincidence? I think not.

Three years later, I refer to my volunteer tribe as my "Rummage Sisters." They were with me from the beginning as I transformed from retired executive to entrepreneur. They continue to be supportive today, and while we only see each other for two months out of the year, we are in contact throughout the year. They are an important part of my network!

Through volunteerism we grow:

1. Our minds by learning new skills and discovering new information about ourselves;
2. Our networks by meeting new people with new interests, and
3. Our hearts by supporting a cause we believe in.

And as we grow, we transform. As Ghandi said, "The best way to find yourself is to lose yourself in the service of others." I say your path rises to meet you. When you find your tribe and lose yourself in the service of others, you will find your path waiting for you to take the next step on your journey of transformation. I know I did.

Deb Wilber is a coach and the owner of Real Life Spark. Whether you are seeking inspiration in your personal life, relationships or career path, her mission is to help you create a plan that will make your goals attainable and find the spark in your life.

www.reallifespark.com

GOALS

Shoot for the moon. Even if you miss,
you'll land among the stars.

– Les Brown

CHAPTER 14

GOAL SETTING DONE RIGHT

BY MARY ILA WARD

It seems as though, as individuals, we often neglect to think strategically about our lives. Thinking about individual purpose both personally and professionally, realizing that both should be intricately intertwined, is where goal setting should begin. Goals direct our actions as individuals, but we need to make sure that these actions are grounded in the bigger picture of who we are and our overall purpose.

DEVELOP A MISSION STATEMENT FIRST

In the corporate world, companies focus on setting strategic plans in order to direct their efforts. Many companies begin with a vision statement and then draft corporate mission and values statements to direct the purpose of their plan. The organization then constantly refers to these guiding statements to determine the goals it sets.

In order to set grounded goals, creating a personal and professional mission statement is imperative. Mission statements should answer the what, how, and why of you. The statement should demonstrate your uniqueness and how you add value, just as a corporate mission statement seeks to do.

One good place to start, in order to brainstorm for a mission statement, is to consider your talents, passions and values. Talents are the things you do well, better than most others. Passions are what crank your tractor, the who, and/or what, that gets you out of bed in the morning and excites you.

Passion is engaging in things that make you lose track of time because you enjoy doing them so much. Values reflect your beliefs about what is important. Making a list of what is important to you, what passions drive you, and what you do better than others, and then incorporating those into a sentence or two to reflect who you are, will define your purpose and thus your mission. Commit this statement to writing and display it in a place where you see it frequently (more than once a day).

GOALS MOTIVATE

Once you have defined your purpose through your mission, goals centered around that mission will drive your success. Research has shown that goal setting, if done correctly, is one of the most supported motivational techniques.

COMMIT IT TO WRITING

Studies have shown those who commit their goals (and of course their mission), in written form, are 9-10 times more successful. The simple act of writing your goals and your mission down prompts action.

Get a journal or notebook and write your mission statement down on the first page. Turn the page and write each goal on the top of the page. Revisit your mission statement and each goal page once a week at a set time to review and reflect on your progress and then write it down.

SET SMART GOALS

A common theme around goal setting is to set "SMART" goals; ones that are:
Specific
Measureable
Attainable
Realistic
Time bound

Evaluating your goals by these standards will help you monitor and achieve your goals successfully.

For example, many people set goals to lose weight. If you simply say your goal is to "lose weight" the likelihood of you doing so is slim. However, if you follow the SMART goals guidelines, and your goal reads more like this, "I will lose 30 pounds in 3 months," making the goal more specific, measurable, attainable and realistic (considering your current weight and health needs), and time bound. You will be much more likely to succeed.

CHANGED BEHAVIORS INDICATE GOAL COMMITMENT

In terms of commitment, honestly examining how committed you are to the goal is important. This can be done by seeing if you can commit to the daily behaviors that will help you reach the goal. Many people fail because the behaviors that lead to goal attainment are not established as habits.

Continuing with the weight loss example, interim behaviors to monitor daily would be to set a calorie intake limit such as "I will consume 1500 calories or less each day" and an exercise goal such as "I will exercise for at least 30 minutes, five days a week." Daily habits that are measurable, in other words, so that at the end of the day you can definitively answer "yes" or "no" to whether or not you followed through on the behavior which will motivate daily performance towards long-term results.

THE LAW OF DIMINISHING RETURNS

At one time or another we all have honestly thought about dozens of different things that we want to accomplish. The law of diminishing returns tells us that the more goals we set, the less likely we are to achieve them. One goal distracts from another, leaving us less likely to accomplish anything.

One good way to avoid this is to have a mission statement and make sure that any goal you set is related to that purpose.

Another way is to answer the two questions that Stephen Covey advocates for asking in his chapter on "Principles of Personal Management" in *The Seven Habits of Highly Effective People*. They are:

Question 1: "What one thing could you do (you aren't doing now) that if you did on a regular basis, would make a tremendous positive difference in your personal life?

Question 2: What one thing in your business or professional life would bring similar results?"

These can be very simple things. The key is, there are only two actions or goals and they are done regularly.

From a leadership perspective, the law of diminishing returns tells us, keep it simple. Too many goals inadvertently tell us that nothing really is important. Nothing gives us all ADD more than too many priorities.

SAY NO

If we want to live purposeful lives and not fall victim to the law of diminishing returns, then we have to say no.

This is easier said than done, but saying no to something is saying yes to something else – namely your mission and the goals you've identified that help you live that mission. There are many worthy and good things to spend time doing. Most of the people I work with that I find are stressed and out of balance aren't the people that are doing irresponsible or "bad" things with their time. They are just stuck in a rut of not knowing how to say no and I believe this is because they haven't defined what is important.

Example 1: A dad finds that he has two to three meetings each week after work related to civic volunteering, church activities, etc. These are all worthy things, but he looks up and realizes he is at home fewer nights a week with his children than he is at another engagement. In defining his purpose and roles, spending quality time with his children is a key priority. He gets off two committees at church but stays on the one that is tied to his mission, commits to only one night a week being available for a work engagement, and signs up to help coach t-ball so he can spend more time with one of his sons.

Example 2: A successful businesswoman has had tremendous success growing her business, but she is now finding herself pulled in too many directions. Because of this, she is leaving the office later and later, waiting until the last minute to get things done, and having a horrible time prioritizing. In addition, she is constantly dealing with a "high maintenance" client that does not pay their bills on time. In addition, the margin on the account isn't even that large. She examines her purpose through drafting a mission statement and develops a plan to delegate certain activities to her employees, based on her desire and purpose to live proactively and align with her purpose to develop others. She has a frank conversation with the "high maintenance" client and lets them know that until they are current on their payments she will not able to follow through on work they want done (again tied to her purpose to live proactively). Quite simply, she turns the ringer on her phone off and closes her email inbox to eliminate distractions when she is working on things that help her live proactively.

Do you have goals done right with:

• A written down mission statement grounded in your talents, passions, and values

• Goals committed to writing, reviewed regularly, and based on your mission

• SMART goals

• Changed behaviors that create habits for goal attainment

• A reasonable number of goals that do not distract from one another (2-5)

• The ability to say no to things because they don't align with your purpose and goals

Mary Ila Ward is the owner of Horizon Point Consulting, Inc. She drives passion in people by helping them connect and grow in careers while helping organizations build a fully engaged workforce that drives productivity. Mary Ila is also a REA Career Consultant.

www.horizonpointconsulting.com

GRIEF

We acquire the strength we have overcome.

– Ralph Waldo Emerson

CHAPTER 15

THE FABULOUS PRINCIPLE©: WHAT WOMEN ENTREPRENEURS KNOW ABOUT LOSS AND TRIUMPH

BY BARBARA RUBEL, M.A., BCETS

Although the warm, bright sun was shining through my hospital window, it was the coldest and darkest day of my life. I was told that my dad killed himself while awaiting the birth of my triplets. Dad shot himself in his head at a time when I was in the hospital about to give birth to three baby boys.

I have found meaning in my loss, have experienced post traumatic growth and learned how to build my resilience. It is often loss that propels women entrepreneurs to become innovative trailblazers, mentors, and leaders. If women are able to find solutions to deal with loss then they can problem solve anything.

My story has propelled me to formulate the FABULOUS Principle© for women entrepreneurs with the understanding that sometimes it is our traumatic losses that become our greatest teacher. This innovative approach is a simple way to enhance resilience. The key to my discovery of the FABULOUS Principle© is the uncovering of eight core competencies that influence women entrepreneurs to grow from their loss experience.

This framework allows leaders to take note of their current stressors such as life events, chronic situations, or perceived work-related threatening conditions in relation to their past losses.

These eight characteristics of resilience (using the acronym F-A-B-U-L-O-U-S) are:

Flexibility: Build a resilient mindset by being less rigid in order to adapt to work-life challenges.

Attitude: A state of mind based on feelings toward certain stressors leaders face in the workplace.

Boundaries: Maintain balance, monitor and maintain limits of acceptable workplace behavior.

Understand Job Satisfaction: Gratification and pleasure gained from a leadership role.

Laughter: Keep a sense of humor to manage a stressful workplace.

Optimism: Think positively, realistically, and anticipate the best possible outcome.

United: Cultivate personal and professional relationships that increase well-being.

Self-compassion: Extend loving kindness to one's self every single day.

Let's take a closer look at each influence of the FABULOUS Principle. Answer 16 questions that generate personal insight by identifying past behaviors that can predict future behaviors as leaders.

FLEXIBILITY

Flexible thinkers can adapt to a changing environment, whether a death related loss or a challenging workplace occurrence. Women entrepreneurs often apply their past knowledge of loss to new situations.

As they exercise leadership, they move away from limiting thought patterns and are open to new ways of learning. It's a fact of life that we learn from our losses. Hence, a past loss challenges the brain to think creatively and problem-solve in order to cope.

With mental agility, adaptability, and resilience, women entrepreneurs don't allow self-limiting tendencies to get in their way.

Looking back: How did my thought process after my loss help me to build my resilience?

Looking ahead: As a flexible thinker, how do I resolve workplace conflicts and manage those who have different communication styles, cultures and beliefs?

ATTITUDE

The Palette of Grief® includes emotional, cognitive, behavioral, physical, and spiritual reactions to loss. There is an art to understanding one's attitudes toward grief reactions. Current outlooks about change are shaped by past loss experiences.

As they struggle with a past loss or evaluate business losses, women entrepreneurs recognize that their feelings, thoughts, and actions are based on their attitude. Therefore, they evaluate their attitude in a positive, negative, or mixed way when they focus on stressors and change.

Looking back: After my loss, how did I handle the changes over which I had no control?

Looking ahead: How does my attitude toward certain people and things facilitate successful leadership?

BOUNDARIES

Being that others may not share the same beliefs, attitudes, or opinions about ways to cope with loss, it's essential to keep personal boundaries in place.

What women entrepreneurs learn from keeping personal boundaries is that these clearly defined limits of behavior protect them from insensitive people who say the wrong thing or expect too much. Likewise, professional boundaries focus on duties, responsibilities, and space.

Disclosing personal information, feeling possessive about a client, or having a romantic relationship with a coworker are boundary violations that can have a long term negative effect. Women entrepreneurs can create organizational policies and get ethics training so they don't go over an established workplace limit or compromise a workplace relationship.

Looking back: After my loss, what obstacles did I face where I had to keep personal boundaries in place?

Looking ahead: What professional boundaries help me to maintain my leadership role?

UNDERSTAND JOB SATISFACTION

The Palette of Grief® can make a person yearn for what was; be frustrated in life; and have an unhappy outlook. For that reason it's important to rely on character strengths to cope.

What women entrepreneurs learn from their loss experience is to continue to use their set of strengths (i.e. authentic, confident, and passionate) to deal with current daily stressors that get in the way of job satisfaction. With an understanding of their strengths, women entrepreneurs acquire the resources they need to do their job well. Namely, they become self-directed leaders who are engaged in the workplace. They are a good fit for the job, satisfied with their role, and emotionally connected to their career.

Looking back: What three strengths helped me to cope with my past loss?

Looking ahead: What three strengths ensure my job satisfaction?

LAUGHTER

After a loss, individuals sometimes feel as though they will never laugh again. In time they learn that keeping a sense of humor enables them to cope. Whether they enjoy stand-up, slapstick, sarcastic, observational, or self-deprecating humor, they realize that humor can get them through difficult times. Women entrepreneurs see the funny side of many workplace challenges. They realize that humor creates laughter and laughter decreases stress. Further, it improves their well-being, enhances their creativity, boosts problem-solving skills, and increases workplace cohesion.

Looking back: After my loss, how was I able to maintain my sense of humor?

Looking ahead: As a leader, in what ways do I incorporate fun into my workplace?

OPTIMISIM

Although loss can bring about hopelessness, an optimistic state of mind can get the bereaved through a difficult point in their lives.

As optimistic leaders reflect on their loss, they remain realistic with sensible expectations and remain hopeful. They are confident in their abilities to manage non-death and death related loss and change. Enthusiastic women entrepreneurs motivate themselves and others. As a rule, they are not only confident in their role, but also passionate about what they do.

Looking back: How was I able to remain hopeful after experiencing a past loss?

Looking ahead: What keeps me hopeful in spite of the impact of current workplace stressors?

UNITED

Although losses can have an enormous impact on relationships, they can help the bereaved to appreciate others and be united and connected with them.

To supervise and foster trust in others, women entrepreneurs manage interpersonal relationships and build rapport. What's more, they recognize their staff and are supportive of them. They know how to give realistic supportive feedback to provide conflict resolution. Leaders recognize the importance of good communication skills as it inspires others.

Moreover, their connections with other women entrepreneurs and perceived social networks are initiators of well-being.

Looking back: What made me feel connected with those who came together to support me after my loss?

Looking ahead: How has peer support, teamwork, networking, or mentorship helped me to become an inspiring leader?

SELF-COMPASSION

Compassion is the caring awareness of another person's difficulties along with the desire to lessen it. Self-compassion is being kind to one's self while problem solving.

To actively find self-soothing activities to alleviate personal distress is crucial after experiencing a loss. As a result, women entrepreneurs continue to extend compassionate loving kindness to themselves while leading others. Self-compassion stimulates women to achieve long-term goals by controlling and regulating negative feelings and impulses.

Rather than negatively appraising their leadership abilities, they create action that focuses on positive outcomes.

Looking back: In what ways was I kind to myself when I felt as though my world was falling apart?

Looking ahead: How does being self-compassionate foster resilience in myself and those I lead?

The question becomes: can our sorrow inspire us to find meaning in our lives as leaders? Self-awareness about one's past experience with grief and personal effectiveness as a leader go hand in hand. Past loss often propels women entrepreneurs into their leadership roles.

The FABULOUS Principle© is a framework for understanding that loss can be a catalyst for positive change and growth, transforming the way women entrepreneurs think about current challenges.

With a flexible mindset and positive attitude, inspirational women maintain their boundaries. They understand ways to maintain job satisfaction, a sense of humor and an optimistic point of view. In essence, leaders recognize the importance of a good network around them and are kind to themselves as they triumph over tragedy.

Barbara Rubel, M.A., BCETS, a keynote speaker on loss and resilience, was featured in an Emmy award documentary. She's the author of But I Didn't Say Goodbye *and* Death, Dying, and Bereavement; *co-author, Dept. of Justice Training Curriculum,* Compassion Fatigue; *contributing writer,* Thin Threads: Grief and Renewal *and* Fresh Grief.

www.griefworkcenter.com

HAPPINESS

Don't put the key to happiness
in someone else's pocket.

– Unknown

CHAPTER 16

YOUR WHY IS YOUR COMPASS FOR HAPPINESS

BY SUZANNE TREGENZA MOORE

I believe that most women have times in their life that they feel a lack of purpose; like they are floating through life and wondering what its meaning is. Many of us feel we are here to serve a higher purpose, but don't take the steps toward figuring out what it is we are meant to do or how "little 'ol me" can do it.

I've felt this way a lot in my life despite doing all the "right things." I graduated from college. I got an MBA. I got married to a nice, tall, handsome man, and had two beautiful little boys. I achieved a six-figure salary.

Despite my charmed path, I didn't feel fulfilled. I always I felt there was something more I was "supposed" to be doing. My task-list for life was missing something.

In many ways, I've found what was missing through entrepreneurship – and the wise mentors I've had who told me to "figure out my BIG WHY." For a while I thought they meant financing my dream of traveling the world extensively, or of buying a house on the lake where I've spent every summer of my life.

Gradually, I learned that these desires were not my BIG WHY. For me – and I don't think I'm alone in this – pursuing something in order to find success with these personal desires only made me feel fulfilled for a short period of time. Conversely, pursuing something in order to find success with a BIG WHY makes me feel fulfilled all of the time.

Think about this for a minute. The best corporations all have mission statements that they share with each and every employee. They strive to do so because when every employee is clear on the mission and on board with it, he or she knows how to behave with customers, vendors, or with each other. There is unity of purpose.

Finding my BIG WHY turned out to be about finding not only my business WHY, but my personal WHY, and the shift that I have experienced since doing so is profound.

Before I found mine, I'd had bouts with depression and anxiety – with no concrete reason for either! Despite being successful by others' measures, I struggled with my work. I was unhappy: feeling that there was something else I should be doing and wanting deeper rewards.

As I developed my entrepreneurial WHY, these struggles gradually melted away. Even the fear I experienced as an entrepreneur became less intense. Instead of focusing on my struggles, I found myself more focused on the anticipated results.

It took a while for me to realize that the entrepreneurial WHY I had developed for my business wasn't JUST about business. My focus on helping other entrepreneurs goes far beyond marketing strategy and coaching. It has to do with how I use my purchasing power, what I share on social media that in no way promotes my business, even what pizza I buy.

My BIG WHY now guides my decisions and is a natural compass for me as to whether something is a fit for me or not. Creating one for yourself can do the same for you.

This can seem like a daunting task. It's the type of thing that by nature many of us would put off, believing it to be a big project we need to "tackle" later. If I were reading this chapter, I can see myself saying: "boy, developing a personal BIG WHY sure seems like a great idea. I'll try to get to that a week from Thursday, but only if nothing else pops up."

Don't worry; mine didn't come to me easily one day in perfect form. It has evolved over time, and although I feel it's pretty snappy now, I know it will continue to do so.

The first iteration was something like: *I want to help moms stay at home with their children if they want and help to support their families.*

This is certainly a respectable start. It led me for quite a while in my business and was a source of inspiration.

Since then it has evolved to: *My Mission is to help other entrepreneurs provide emotionally, physically, spiritually, and financially for those they love, by creating, marketing, and running successful businesses.*

126

This speaks to me in a more complete way. There is clarity in it that didn't exist earlier.

If you are feeling as though developing a BIG WHY – personal or business - would be helpful to you, here are a few steps you can take to create it.

STEP 1: HOW ARE YOU SERVING OTHERS?

First, take a moment to think about how you are now or want to be serving people in your life and, if you have one, in your business. Often we don't recognize all of those that benefit from our activities.

I know personally, I've done things like volunteer in my children's classes because I enjoy seeing them in their learning environment.

I forget that some of the children don't have parents willing or able to do the same: that my kindness toward them can have real meaning in their lives. There are some who aren't told how great they are or what beautiful artwork they've made.

And in business, especially when I was a virtual assistant, sometimes it was hard to recognize that writing email content for a client served a larger purpose. Today, knowing those emails led dozens of women to enter programs that helped solve challenges is very meaningful to me.

Take some time, a week or two, to look at your daily activities and work – especially the parts that you enjoy – and look at the bigger picture of who they are serving and how you could expand on that to uncover your BIG WHY.

Write your activities down. Journal about them. Discuss what you are trying to uncover with a friend or partner.

Then ask yourself:

• Who beyond those I love is being served by what I do/how I spend my time?

• Why is that important to me?

• How can I continue to make a difference for the community that is being served?

• How does this serve others beyond what I can see?

• What actions could I take to make what I'm doing more impactful?

STEP 2: WHAT MAKES YOU FEEL SUCCESSFUL?

A number of years ago, when I was trying to figure out the direction of my business, a wonderful friend and coach asked me what the best days of work had looked like for me. We were focused on work activities, but the same question applies whether you are in business or not. What makes you feel great at the end of a day: like you've been of service, really helped someone, used your unique brilliance?

I'm going to challenge you to identify AT LEAST five activities that you do and that you enjoy that make you feel successful and as though you are working using *your unique gifts.*

I'm challenging you to five because our tendency is to cut ourselves off after one or two.

Write these down so you have them in front of you

STEP 3: CREATE YOUR FIRST BIG WHY STATEMENT

Now let's take a look at what you have after working through Steps 1 & 2. Think about how you are serving others, and what makes you feel successful.

Your BIG WHY lives somewhere inside of them.

From your writings thus far, I want you to develop a statement about what your BIG WHY is. This may come very easily for you, or it may take some time. As I mentioned earlier, mine came to me in a general way a number of years ago, but I keep refining it and making it more specific as I go deeper into my work.

Take some time to think about yours. Noodle around with it in your head a little bit. Don't sit over a piece of paper trying to write it down. Go for a walk and enjoy the sunshine while you are thinking about it.

But do take the time to think about it, and when you feel you have the beginnings of it, write it down. Put a sign up in your office, or your kitchen, or your studio…wherever you spend the most time so that you can be reminded what you are really working for.

As changes to it come to you, refine it. Some day you will feel that it is the compass you need to keep you on track and live a life of purpose.

Suzanne Tregenza Moore is an online marketing strategist and host of the podcast, Advancing Entrepreneur. Guiding clients through the steps of her Simplify Online Marketing™ system, she is fulfilling her mission to enable other entrepreneurs to serve more clients while providing for their families emotionally, physically, spiritually, and financially.

www.SuzanneTMoore.com

MANIFESTING

Life isn't about finding yourself.
Life is about creating yourself.
– George Bernard Shaw

CHAPTER 17

CONSCIOUSLY OR UNCONSCIOUSLY, YOU WILL CREATE

BY RICHARD PERRO

As a life coach, one of the first concepts that I discuss with my clients is that we create the lives we are experiencing. Therefore, this vital knowing, when accepted and understood, enables us to create the lives we truly desire. This crucial step and shift in awareness, once realized, allows us to redirect our energy in a positive manner.

Ironically, the one constant in life is that life is constantly changing. We are always making choices; yet how many of us are consciously aware that our thoughts and actions are normally derived from the super or subconscious mind? Every action we take runs through this filter of the mind and our decisions are based on which emotion is presently stronger, love or fear. Through this process of the mind creation is born.

What is creation? Creation is an action that represents what a person believes and the by-product of all the experiences that manifest from those beliefs. Once created, certain things are evident and cannot be devoid of responsibility. If we are overweight and unhappy with our physical appearance, we can usually trace it back to poor food habits or a lack of discipline when it pertains to exercise. The law of cause and effect is quite clear here in this example, but unfortunately most of us are unconscious to the drives that direct us.

As children, our view of the world is a reflection of those who have nurtured us in our early stages of development. This critical imprinting is subject to the map of reality presented by those who cared for us. Beliefs are then accepted as truth, until we can discover proof to the contrary. Unfortunately, many of us do not challenge the data received which can limit our spectrum of opportunities. So the age old adage, "the rich get richer and the poor get poorer" is not a rule but simply a reinforced thought. Given the fact that all nurtured beings are conditioned in one form or another it is imperative that we understand the concept of conscious creation.

When an individual has dreams and aspirations they need to also ask themselves if the true desire behind this inspiration is good. This is where the challenges may arise. In a world of infinite possibilities, you must possess the courage to attach yourself to your dream, qualify it as good, and do whatever is necessary to see it through.

To be disciplined or the way of the disciple, takes more than intention, it also takes tenacity. Are you foundationally sound and prepared for the task? If someone wants to be a doctor and yet they have no tolerance for science, is this a dream that this person will eventually hold on to? In creation, one is either creating from the I or the me. The I and the me when realized will be the test that determines if something is good for us; if we are truly honest with ourselves.

Personally one of my dreams has been to be a writer because it is what I love to do and it allows me to share my inspired thoughts in a loving way which I hope will benefit others. My statement here is in agreement because my desire is driven by love and service to others and I can hold onto this dream because there are no conflicting motivations.

In a different scenario, a person may say I want to be a doctor because my father is a doctor and he will be proud of me. The I and the me in this statement do not agree. It does not mean that there is something wrong with this, nor does it mean that he or she would not be a good doctor if they follow through with it. In creation there are many roads to bliss if you have the courage to travel the paths of uncertainty. However, the greatest chance of seeing a dream materialize is when it is inspired for the love of the work and service to others and not motivated by secondary gains or fear.

All motivations may not always be so easily reconciled. An individual who owns a business that has been the industry standard for decades may face the challenge of new technologies that create opportunities to meet the needs in a cheaper and more environmentally friendly way. This person now has the choice to say I must change the direction of my business to support the new advancements and the environment because it is the right thing to do or I will oppose the changes because of the fear of losing my market share.

The motivations behind these examples were completely different. Ultimately, the choice one makes will determine which state they are creating from....love or fear and are they even consciously aware of it?

Creation has qualifiers which are required to achieve one's goals. Qualifiers are certain demands on the noun or verb that formulate distinction. Qualifiers vary from culture to culture and are defined by the standards that we have culturally agreed upon. Even happiness, when displayed without an obvious reason, may beckon qualification. You see the true gift of creation is to design things that suit us. The law of attraction is depleted tremendously when we apply conditions on our happiness.

Example: A person wants to be a dancer. Dancer is a noun. Most people can dance in some capacity or another. Would the sheer love of dancing (verb) satisfy the desire to be a dancer (noun)? This depends on all of the supposed qualifiers. If one believes that nothing but being the prima ballerina in a world renowned ballet company would satisfy their definition of a professional dancer, then the likelihood of this extremely qualified dream has been laden greatly with conditions. To be revered as the best and nothing less will satisfy may be motivated by the ego. This demand is hard to satisfy because even if this goal were attained, how long can this projection of the best be maintained in an ever-changing environment?

Once we truly examine the conditions placed upon the creation we can determine the likelihood of the experience being realized as defined by us. Does this mean our personal qualifiers should determine the definition of dancer for all?

Certainly not!

Does this mean that a person should not go after the dream of being a professional dancer if they don't meet all the qualifiers? Absolutely not! It will take lot of hard work, courage and perseverance. If the dream to dance is stronger than the qualifiers then something within the dance world of an equal love shall present itself because as Paulo Coelho said, "when you want something, the universe conspires in helping you to achieve it."

In creation, as in life there are no certainties, only experiences which require perspective, inner resolve, and conscious choice. All is good because everything created has a purpose when we love and accept the creation without qualifications. Reconciling our fears and making peace with our qualifiers will allow us to transform our limiting beliefs; and consciously create from an I that serves from love and not the me that is based in fear. This frees us to be the creators that we were all born to be.

Richard Perro is a life coach whose areas of expertise include astrology, tarot, numerology, and astrotheology. Richard incorporates these disciplines to help clients understand their path in life and facilitate the knowing that all experiences are gifts once seen in the proper perspective.

www.richardperro.com

MENTAL FITNESS

It's not the mountain we conquer but ourselves.
– Edmund Hillary

CHAPTER 18

THE ART OF MENTAL FITNESS

BY S.E. HICKMAN, Ph.D., Psy.D.

Tasha is an attractive, 48-year-old highly successful female executive. Married for 28 years, she and her husband have two daughters, Calista and Maverick, who are both in college. Her punishing gym routine sculpts her 5'4" frame to a neat 130 pounds and she can be found daily in her office by 7:30 am, tidying her glass-topped desk as she prepares for another meeting-laden day. To all accounts, Tasha is a happy, well-adjusted individual, beautifully fitted with the accouterments of success.

What you would not know is that Tasha frequently vomits into the toilet of her private bathroom and suffers gut-wrenching bouts of self-criticism. Although well-liked by coworkers and described by friends as "cheerful and sociable," Tasha feels desperately alone as her inner critic taps out a steady drumbeat of demands. In response, Tasha further tightens her emotional reigns, demanding an ever-increasing level of productivity and perfection.

Surprisingly, Tasha's story is not all that unusual. In reality, our modern society compels ambitious people to develop highly targeted skills in some areas such as career and income, while almost completely ignoring others, such as mental and emotional fitness.

While relationships are a hot topic in pop culture, this is often limited to the context of failed relationships and smarmy advice on how to "get what you want" from your partner, which is little more than thinly veiled attempts at self-fulfillment through manipulation.

Physical fitness and weight loss are popular topics as well, but a quick glance around would suggest there are major impediments to the health goals of our nation. With so much time invested in chasing the dollar, quality relationships and physical health fall rapidly down the list of priorities. What slot is left, then, for mental and emotional fitness? Well, that horse is not even in the line-up.

THE TARNISHING OF MENTAL HEALTH

Unfortunately, most people primarily think of mental issues in the negative; that is, in terms of instability and illness, hence the reason that the term *mental health* has literally become synonymous with *mental illness*.

The vast majority of individuals still consider seeking mental health services as shameful and to be avoided. Historically, this in part stems from the assignment of emotions as primarily feminine, corresponding to the stereotype that women are naturally emotional while men are naturally rational. Thus, women are allowed to express emotions, while men are generally discouraged from doing so, except perhaps anger or jealousy. Thus, mental states have been historically ignored in terms of daily functioning. A few exceptions exist, such as in sports and business arenas where mental states have been considered for enhancing success or performance.

This is not to ignore that fields such as sociology and psychology have been dedicated to the study of mental, social, and emotional processes. However, the study of "objective behavior" was initially highly favored over "subjective" experiences, which were disregarded as irrelevant except as it related to clinical disorders. Fortunately, the tide is slowing turning as movements such as positive psychology and psychoneurobiology have begun to recognize that subjective experiences profoundly impact and co-construct our reality.

INTRODUCING MENTAL FITNESS

For all of these reasons, I discard the term *mental health* altogether as it is hopelessly entangled in the quagmire of *mental illness*. Instead, I propose the term mental fitness. I believe the majority of mental disorders actually stem from accumulated skill deficits across time rather than representing an innate disorder.

For example, young adults diagnosed with anxiety frequently have parents with anxiety, which means *how to be anxious* was routinely modeled rather than *how to successfully cope* with anxiety-provoking situations. Regardless of genetic contributions, this context would lead to skills deficits.

Let's explore at least a working definition of mental fitness and then consider each component in turn:

To be mentally fit is to have practiced and insightful awareness of our mental and emotional states - particularly as it relates to holistic mental, emotional, social, physical, financial, and spiritual functioning - and to have resilient and adaptive control over these states through acquired skills whether in stress or at rest, including the developed ability to harness and flexibly use these states in responsible service to our goals while balancing personal welfare with the welfare of others.

First, *practiced and insightful awareness* suggests that we develop the skill to step back and examine why (and when) we experience certain thoughts and emotions and how this impacts overall functioning. Otherwise, we will largely *react* to our circumstances based on our internalized beliefs (functional or dysfunctional) rather than being able to thoughtfully *act*. As long as we merely react, we are slaves to circumstance and in the absence of practiced awareness, there is no possibility of change.

Second, *resilient and adaptive control over these states through acquired skills whether in stress or at rest* is to say that regardless of the context, whether stressful or relaxed, we are able to shape and control thoughts and emotions in service to our goals without abdicating responsibility through avoidance. Importantly, we must recognize that skills rarely happen naturally but are acquired through practice.

Third, the *developed ability to harness and flexibly use these states in responsible service* to our goals means learning how to use awareness to adapt to contextual demands through deliberate and careful action. Just as flexible bodies suffer less damage in rigorous activity, cognitively flexible individuals suffer less emotional and mental damage under duress. We must learn how to *do what is effective* in reaching goals, rather than what our emotions or thoughts might naturally drive us toward.

Finally, flexibility also entails *balancing personal welfare with the welfare of others.* To myopically pursue self-interest with disregard to the needs and feelings of others is to provoke social and relational chaos, which in turn impacts us negatively. To ignore the spiritual law of reciprocity is to invite disaster.

THE ART OF MENTAL FITNESS: SEVEN SECRETS FOR MASTERY

Mental fitness mastery requires consistent practice to solidify the skills. Be patient with yourself and enlist the help of others when you are unable to see things clearly. While there are many different skills, here are seven fundamental ones:

1. Observe Your Patterns. To eliminate avoiding and raise awareness, keep this simple log for 30 days. For each upsetting event, describe: 1) the event, 2) emotional responses, 3) associated thoughts, 4) behavioral responses and consequences, and 5) rate response effectiveness from 1 (least) to 10 (most). Example from Tasha:

• Event: Criticized by boss.

• Emotion: Shame, anger, sadness.

• Thoughts: "I'll never get that promotion," and "Everyone thinks I am incompetent."

• Behavior: Overate then threw up.

• Effectiveness: 3 – Felt better temporarily, but then felt worse.

2. Insightfully Plan Alternative Behaviors. Learn to *act* rather than *react.* For negative thoughts in your log, develop and practice challenge statements and devise more adaptive responses. Over time, new patterns will replace old ones. Most people react first and only later become curious about their reactions. Insight-driven behavior reverses the order by being curious first, then selecting a desirable response. An example from Tasha:

• I'll never get a promotion was replaced with My hard work will pay off in the end.

• Action Choice: Rather than binging and purging, Tasha noted the need for comfort and journaled her thoughts and emotions, exercised vigorously to reduce stress and then called a close friend for support.

3. Recognize, Accept and Satisfy Emotional Needs. Expressing emotions in healthy ways keeps us balanced. Emotions merely signify needs, which must be addressed, not denied or avoided. Give yourself permission to have needs and don't waste energy on judging them. Focus on fulfilling your needs in a healthy way. Ultimately, emotions will *not* be denied. Ignored emotions often result in physical illness.

4. Artfully Use Emotions. Master the art of purposefully evoking emotions for specific goals. For example, if classical music inspires your novel writing, play it! Find and hang out with people who inspire your success. Stop fighting your emotions and harness them for your advantage. By purposefully evoking positive emotional states, you can learn to *switch* from negative to positive states at will rather than being held captive by them.

5. Develop Mental and Emotional Flexibility. Based on prior experience and developmental context, everyone develops a set of patterned responses. These routinized responses can make us feel stuck. To increase flexibility, force a change in your routines: 1) do the opposite of any ritualized behavior, 2) purposefully interrupt your favorite activities, 3) delay gratification, 4) let others win an argument, 5) let others lead, and 6) seek alternative perspectives to your own.

6. Do What is Effective. Injustice is everywhere, but we must accept *what* is rather than demanding what *ought to be* or we ultimately forfeit effectiveness. For example, Tasha may experience anger over her father's criticism and is certainly justified because she deserves acceptance. However, she can't embrace self-acceptance and allow others to love her until she accepts her father's limitations, realizing it has little to do with her personally and everything to do with him. Self-acceptance is effective for mental fitness; holding on to anger is not.

7. Practice Good Community. No man is an island, no matter how alone he feels. Community cannot be avoided, so we must practice good community by investing in others. We are each called to a purpose, one that both gives and receives and our contribution to collective happiness is the only meaningful thing we can leave behind. Money is spent. Buildings crumble. Love, however, never fades and can be passed down indefinitely.

Remember, mental fitness is a skills-based art and requires practice for mastery. Begin your mental fitness journey today!

S. E. Hickman, Ph.D., Psy.D., is a psychologist, transformational coach, and entrepreneur. Founder of the Mental Fitness Institute, she is passionate about mental fitness and writes extensively in the field. She enjoys serving as a psychological expert for television, radio, and print media.

www.DrSusanHickman.com.

NURTITION

The body is a perfect reflection of the
choices you make over a lifetime. Knowledge
is important, but adding more good advice isn't
the solution to healthy eating. The solution
is to transform your awareness.

– Deepak Chopra, MD

CHAPTER 19

SEE, FEEL, TASTE, AND EXPERIENCE YOUR FOOD – EMBRACE CONSCIOUS EATING

BY CARYN O'SULLIVAN

What if you were able to eat anything you wanted without the threats of gaining weight, over eating, feeling guilty, or getting sick? For some, that would be an invaluable gift to break the chains of food addiction, emotional eating, and illness.

Food means many things to people. Food is comfort, pleasure, fun, a means of zoning out, finding solace in an overwhelming world, or a way to hide. Food is also associated with shame, failure, accomplishment, or success. In today's modern world, the purpose of food surpasses nourishment or energy for the body. Because of this complexity, food can be confusing!

The good news is we all have the ability to eat without confusion, discomfort, or guilt. The secret lies with Conscious Eating.

Conscious Eating is engaging in any form of eating, but being present in mind, body, and spirit. It is paying attention to what you are eating, how much you are eating, how you are eating, and why you are eating. It is being aware of your food, and how it was grown, made, or produced. Conscious Eating is taking note of how you feel before, during, and after eating, and connecting the dots between cravings and eating habits.

Conscious eating could be the most important thing you can do for your body, for your health, and for this planet. It is also the most difficult, as we live in a society where productivity and efficiency are valued more than relaxation and concentration; where the family meal is in danger of extinction, and many people do not spend time in the kitchen cooking anymore. To put it simply, we don't have the time to eat, but yet we eat so much. However, how much of the food that we put into our mouths do we actually taste? And are we eating for hunger or another reason?

As a health coach, I repeatedly see people who dislike food, are afraid of food, don't care about food, or use food as a means to control their world. These are not healthy relationships, but destructive ones.

In the Western World we have so much food – an abundance of food really, that it is no longer used for nourishment or celebration. Instead, this surplus encourages overeating, binging, denying ourselves, and being wasteful. We can eat all day and not really be aware of what we are eating, why we are eating, or what it is doing to our bodies. It is this disconnect that encourages unhealthy habits.

HOW DO WE EAT CONSCIOUSLY?

We are all born with the ability to eat consciously. In fact, if you watch a baby eat, he/she knows just how much to eat each at meal and when to stop. A baby who is full will simply turn her head to one side, purse her lips together, or swat your hand away. She will not eat if full or feeling ill. Unfortunately, as we grow older we "reprogram" ourselves to eat beyond fullness. This reprogramming often surfaces in three ways:

1. Parents often encourage kids to clean their plates, or give praise (or dessert) if they eat everything. This causes one to learn how to ignore what I call the "fullness factor," - a critical insight that helps to prevent overeating and weight issues.

2. At a young age, we pick up bad habits from parents or others to eat when we are not hungry - yielding to boredom, sadness, anger, peer pressure, or other emotional or social reasons.

3. We are encouraged to snack throughout the day, rather than focus on three balanced meals. Often these snacks are processed, not nutrient dense, full of preservatives and/or salt and fat, leaving your body seeking the nutrients and in turn, asking for more food. To eat consciously, we need to reprogram our bodies to tap that intuition we are all born with. It is inside you!

Now that you know what conscious eating is, how do you begin? Follow these seven steps below and you will be on your way.

Sit down while you eat. Many people eat on the run, compromising digestion and ending up with bloat, gas, or other stomach ailments. Meals are meant to be savored and are a life experience. When we sit down to eat, our stomach is in a relaxed posture and our awareness is on the taste, texture, and smell of the food.

We are more likely to engage all our senses and eat slower. There's an old Ayurveda saying, "If you eat standing up, death looks over your shoulder." Sitting down while eating can be challenging, so take it one meal at a time.

Chew your food. Digestion actually begins in the mouth by engaging enzymes in your saliva. The more you chew, the less work your stomach and intestines have to do. Also, chewing slows you down, so you actually TASTE your food. As a result, you may become aware of actual likes/dislikes.

For instance, a chocolate cupcake just eaten in a few bites without any awareness may seem like it tastes good, and you may have a few more. However, if you actually chew it and taste every bit of it, you may realize you don't like it at all. This was the case for one of my clients. She ate the same chocolate cake every day after work while walking to the train station. When she sat down and chewed it, however, she realized she didn't like it at all!

Eat without distractions. In today's fast paced world, sitting at the table and actually eating a meal undisturbed just seems impossible! We are constantly distracted by television, smart phones, books, newspapers, etc. To just focus on eating may seem boring or a waste of time.

Many cultures around the world still place a strong emphasis on food as the main event of the day. In France or Spain, lunchtime is a full course meal that lasts a couple hours and is eaten slowly. In the United States, grabbing a sandwich and eating while working or eating on the run is more the usual custom.

Mindless eating contributes to obesity, digestive disorders, energy issues, and emotional eating.

Slow down! Constantly being on the run keeps us in a state of stress. Your food cannot be digested properly while you are stressed because the sympathetic, or "fight or flight," nervous system is triggered.

In this state, your body doesn't know the difference between casual day-to-day stress and running away from a tiger! So, it discontinues all digestive processes to give you more energy to fight or to flee.

Eating should, however, trigger your parasympathetic nervous system, which is calming and releases digestive enzymes, bile, and blood flow to the digestive tract. Obviously, your food will be received much better when you are calm than when you are stressed. Many digestive disorders are caused by eating at the wrong time or too quickly.

Put your fork down in between bites. Putting your fork down in between bites could be your ticket to conscious eating. It makes you stop and chew, as well as breathe in between bites. Eating slowly allows your digestive system to get started and not be overwhelmed by shovels of food. Slow down, fork down, breathe and chew. Your stomach will thank you!

Stop eating when full. Within each of us, there is an alarm that goes off when we have eaten too much. No, we are not going to hear this alarm, but it is a gentle signal from the body to stop eating. If we have gone past that point, we will feel bloated or uncomfortable.

The "fullness factor" comes to us as a feeling of satiation or of gentle pressure in the abdomen. If you are not eating consciously, you will easily miss this alarm.

Give thanks before a meal. Being grateful promotes healthy digestion! Eating while upset often results in gas and bloating, constipation or loose stools – even if you are eating healthy foods! Saying grace before a meal allows you to take a step back from your busy day, change your mindset, and focus on the positive. Your stomach will be grateful in return.

In conclusion, we can learn a lot from our bodies if we stopped to listen. Your health journey, and mine, is much more than just what you put in your mouth. The *how and when* play important roles as well, as does your lifestyle, attitude and emotional state.

I challenge you to eat consciously. Sit, without distractions. Smell your food. See with your eyes, feel with your hands, taste with your mouth. Experience, don't just go through the motions.

Conscious eating is the key to a healthy life. It teaches you to be aware in your life and of your decisions; to be respectful of your body; to be grateful for food and the process of farm to table; to be mindful of every bite; and to consciously choose to love who God made you to be!

Caryn O'Sullivan is a Health Coach and founder of Appetites for Life, LLC. Trained at the Institute of Integrative Nutrition and with a certificate in Chinese Dietary Therapy, Caryn supports women who want a positive connection with food by encouraging conscious and mindful eating.

www.appetitesforlife.com

PAIN

We must embrace pain and
burn it as fuel for our journey.
– Kenji Miyazawa

CHAPTER 20

STOP RUNNING FROM YOUR PAIN

BY RUSCHELLE SMIROLDO-KHANNA, LCSW

Pain is an essential element of being human. It is the diamond pillar of our intuition. Intuition is the innate ability to respond to our surroundings in the present moment, without thinking and often with the purpose of saving our lives. No matter how it comes, through the storm of heartbreak or the overwhelm of physical pain, whether we like it or not, it is here to guide us into our next phase of life.

On March 3, 2014, I walked home from the gym with a bit of a pain in my neck. My 115-pound frame was strong and healthy. I felt really good, minus the neck pain: Maybe I wasn't stretching enough.

Ten hours later began a nine-day spiral of seizures and the onset of dystonia (inability to control muscles) that would last for over a month. The dystonia was only the beginning. Little did I know that my body would endure multiple neurological symptoms ranging from vision and hearing loss to psychosis. I was terrified.

As I lie writhing in pain day after day, without answers from Western medicine, I planned to die. In my suffering I began to pray. As I prayed, a phrase came to me. "I am amazing and amazed," some inner voice said. "Why would I say that?" I thought. But the answer shortly followed. Somehow the pain had thrust me into an overwhelming state of awareness and clarity. I was fully present. I was more than present.

I WAS the present.

I was amazing because I had survived such an intense experience and I was amazed at the shear experience of life itself.

Thus began my journey to not only find out what had happened to me but to make sense of it...if I could. I was only capable of making "in the moment" decisions. Which way should I turn to be out of pain? When will the next attack hit? How will I prepare myself?

The definition of intuition is the ability to understand something immediately, without the need for conscious reasoning. Essentially, intuition is being in the present and acting accordingly. My pain experience allowed me the opportunity to wake up to my life more fully than I ever imagined. And it saved my life. We are all born with an incredible ability to sift through information instantly. However, it, just like intellect, can be honed and refined.

WRITING YOUR PAIN STORY

Pain is an experience that can either drive us fully into the present or motivate us to run away through the use of drugs or other distractions. But it really is up to us to decide which way to go. In the case of my neurological Lyme disease, I chose the first. I chose to deny the idea that I had a Lyrica deficiency or that I "should not be in pain." Well why not experience pain? The pain was my guide and meter to know whether or not I was healing. Why would I want to turn that off?

I am not just referring to physical pain. This can also be psychological. Whatever it is it must emotionally charge you to the point that your full attention is brought into the present. Anger is a perfect example. Our rage has the ability to either drive us into full presence or blind us so completely that we act without any awareness at all.

Physical pain is the same. I experienced physical pain unbearable to the point of wanting to end my life. Amazingly, that same pain has given me the ability to cultivate the confidence to do pretty much anything I can set my mind to.

To start new businesses, try new things, to inspire others. What is your pain point? Can you access it? In what ways can you start expressing it? I chose to write.

GO AHEAD, ENJOY IT

By July of 2014 I had been to multiple physicians, including several emergency visits. Nothing came out of it. My primary physician insisted I needed Klonopin and Lyrica, both of which I refused. Dr. Google kept saying that I either had MS or mercury poisoning. Since I had already been tested for MS and there was no reliable test for mercury toxicity, I went ahead and joined the "mercury poisoned" group on Facebook.

I followed the advice of some of the strangers from the group, after all, I did have three mercury fillings. I began basic detox and health protocols including high doses of vitamin C and magnesium. The pain reduced, I prayed some more. I begged for my pain to go away and could no longer work.

I could hardly crawl away from my continually running Epsom bath. I cried day and night. Finally I wrote my symptoms and posted to the group. I asked if anyone knew what I might have beyond mercury toxicity. Five people responded that I had Lyme. I then called every Lyme office I could. I visited two. I was tested and it was spot on. I had an answer and began treatment. Although the pain reduced, it still lingered.

October came and I returned from visiting my parents. While I was in their home, I had three debilitating pain attacks. I would cry uncontrollably. They really had no idea what to do with me. All I could keep thinking was, "I have to find a way to get this pain under control." I kept saying to myself "It is my body, there has to be a way I can control this." Then it dawned on me that maybe I should just try to start really feeling the sensation and somehow enjoying it.

That Monday when I returned back to the city, I called my prayer partner. For some reason I felt I needed to run this crazy idea past someone. Essentially I asked her if she thought it would be okay if I try somehow enjoying my pain the next time it happened. Her response was, "Well you are suffering so much and it is your body, so I say do whatever you have to, to feel better."

Utter joy and an almost giddy sensation swelled up inside me. I ended the phone call wanting a pain attack to hit just to see what I could do with it.

Your pain can thrust you into the present moment. Your pain can paralyze you or call you to action. I encourage you to own it, make it yours, befriend it and use to your advantage.

Yes there are still days when I just want it to go away for good, days when I just don't want to deal with hurting. But ultimately I have decided that I was given the gift of ultimate present awareness, confidence, and motivation that I never had acquired after years of meditating. Has there ever been a painful moment in your life that you tried to enjoy for the sake of being alive?

OWNING IT

Owning my pain forced me into radical self-care. There comes a point when you hurt so bad that you just refuse to let anyone else hurt you. It's called a pain threshold and for me this was a fantastic thing to discover.

Essentially I was in so much pain physically and emotionally that I would be damned if I let another person inflict any type of pressure on me. The result - one self-confident piece of work. I realized my previously unknown lack of self-confidence.

The main takeaway from an illness that fills us with rage is that you are worth yelling, screaming and pushing people out of the way. It could very well save your life. No one else is going to take up for you in that way.

My back is still on fire some days. I own it. My body is doing an incredible job fighting an infection. I appreciate it and all its warning signs. I try to roll around in the sensation of having a spine and a nervous system that can feel, while modifying my life to feel better. I express my pain through writing, advocating, and being around people that appreciate someone being real. I use this to fuel my own desire to find a cure and inspire others. Ironically, pain, as unwanted as it is, cuts through the nonsense. It allows you get right to the point of your life.

No one, myself included, necessarily wants to be in pain. That said, if someone asked that I remove the physical pain, hardship brought on by Lyme disease and along with it they would take my newfound confidence, loving connections and joy for life, I would clearly say, I will keep my pain. It's my pain. I own it and can do exactly as I please with it.

Ruschelle Smiroldo-Khanna, LCSW, is a psychotherapist and women's health advocate in Manhattan. Ruschelle has helped thousands of women regain health and vitality. She combines personal experience and a decade of professional experience to empower women to take control of their health.

www.simplybeconsulting.com.

PARENTING

Don't handicap your children
by making their lives easy.

– Robert A. Heinlein

CHAPTER 21

GOOD INTENTIONS IN PARENTING AND THE ROAD TO HELL AND BACK

BY FERN WEIS

"If I only knew then what I know now." I can't tell you how many times I've heard that from parents (and how many times I said it myself). We tend to put up with a lot until we just can't stand it anymore, and find our family in a jam, or worse. We have the best of intentions, but those intentions can lead us astray, away from what's really in our family's best interest. You've heard the expression, "The road to hell is paved with good intentions." There is a way back, and there's also a way to avoid going there altogether. Let's get started.

One of the things I learned during my child's trial-by-fire teen years was that caring and good intentions weren't enough. They were actually part of the problem. It took some work to come to terms with where I had gone wrong, and to accept that I was still a good person. This quote sums it up: "Intentions! You can have them. They can be pure and good. In your mind you will execute them in a very precise manner with the purest of hearts. Then something happens and shoots it all to hell. Does that make a person any less good? I don't think it does." (Michelle Gable)

Here's how it goes. Your family is doing all right, there are no crises looming. You're all chugging along. And then one day you wake up and ask yourself, "How did we get here?" Now there are some issues: disrespect, slipping grades, defiant behaviors, drinking, breaking curfew, depression.

How did you get there? There are many reasons you can find yourself on the bad road of good intentions, such as a desire for peace and quiet, over-giving to your children, or excessive pressure about grades.

You may not trust them to make good decisions, or it's difficult to watch them experience sadness or disappointment. You're afraid they'll make mistakes that can't be fixed, and so you fix things for them. It can also be difficult to accept that life isn't fitting the image you had when you started your family.

That ideal image is tough to let go. (I also want to be clear that you are not responsible for everything your children do. They made choices along the way; however, they had some help from you in becoming who they are now.) You want things to go smoothly... but that's not always the best approach to take.

Here are two examples of my own good intentions gone awry with my kids.

After my son was back on track, he explained to me how my intervening actually sent the message that I didn't believe in him. This was before I 'woke up' to my misguided good intentions. He had learning issues that required some modifications in class. During his turbulent high school years, at the yearly re-evaluation meeting, I asked for some expectations to be lowered in the hopes that he would experience more success. What he heard was, "You can't do it. You're not capable." This was a real eye-opener for me. Without using those words, I had said all that. I had contributed to lowering his self-esteem, exactly the opposite of what I wanted to accomplish.

My daughter also had to set me straight. She had moved overseas to study and required our assistance co-signing a lease. As the move-in date drew closer, I asked her several times if she had received the signed leases from her roommates' parents. What a surprise when she replied, "Mom, I wasn't worried before... but now you're making me nervous, and wondering if I should be worried." Again, my anxiety, my feeling that things were out of my control, was sending the message that she couldn't handle things on her own, and increased her anxiety. These were not my finest moments.

We parents send messages we aren't aware of, through our words, actions, emotional responses, and body language. We are constantly communicating to our children how we see ourselves, the world, and our place in it. How do you find your way back and do right by your kids?

Pay attention to that little voice or sensation in your body, the one that's telling you something isn't quite right. What's going on with your child?

What does that bring up for you? You have a great deal of wisdom, and it is sometimes pushed aside by your fears. That little voice is telling you to pay attention, to take a look at what's going on.

Accept that there is a situation or behavior that needs attention and action. Not all problems turn into a crisis, but they are still warrant closer examination. And remember, intervention is the best prevention. This means that taking an action has the potential to prevent a situation from getting worse. Keep in mind that your action is not to fix it for your child. It may be to listen, guide, encourage, set a boundary or limit, or ask someone else for help.

Share it with someone you trust - a spouse or partner, another family member, or a professional who can guide you through it. I know firsthand how difficult it is to put words to it; to admit that there's something too big to handle yourself; that maybe you made mistakes; and the embarrassment that you and your kids are struggling when everyone else seems to have it together (which they don't, because everybody has something they're dealing with).

I remember that when I found the courage to voice my deepest fears and regrets, they took on a life of their own and became real. They were no longer my secret. That was scary, and yet a good thing. Once I put it out there, there was no turning back. I had to act... which leads us to #4.

Take action, even imperfect action. Nothing changes until you do. If you wait until you're standing at the edge of a cliff, your options are limited. So do something, sooner rather than later. Resist the perfection demon, the one that says you must have everything planned out, all the steps lined up and ready to go. Many people get stuck here, and lose sight of the bigger picture of what needs to be accomplished. You need a first step. The rest will follow.

This is the way back. Don't wait for a little unpleasantness to turn into a big problem. Examine your motivation for getting involved. Be aware and proactive. Share and take a step to break those unproductive habits and attitudes, so you can all be your best, unique, amazing selves.

REFLECTION/ACTION QUESTIONS

• How were success and failure handled during your growing-up years?

• What were some of the 'failures' you experienced, and what did you learn from them?

• Think of a time when you intervened to 'fix' a situation for your child. What was your motivation? What did he learn about how to deal with life's challenges?

• Make a list of your child's strengths. Ask your child what he thinks his strengths are. Compare your lists and celebrate!

• Have a conversation. Ask your child what messages he's heard from you. What does he want from you when he faces a challenge? Sometimes all he needs is to vent so he can clear his head and begin to problem-solve. Other times he needs help. Talk about it.

Fern Weis is a Parent Coach, Family Recovery Coach, and the mother of two amazing young adults. She specializes in supporting parents who are going through difficult situations with their teen and young adult children, including addiction recovery.

www.fernweis.com

PERSEVERANCE

All the world's a stage and all the
men and women merely players. They
have their exits and their entrances.
– William Shakespeare

CHAPTER 22

THE SHOW MUST GO ON

BY CARYN CHOW

The year was 1991 – a most significant one because it marked the last time I delivered a monologue on a theatrical stage, and the last year I spent with "Poh Poh," my beloved maternal grandmother.

Earlier that year, I auditioned for the lead role in the Off-Broadway premiere of "Letters to a Student Revolutionary," a play documenting the friendship of two women who ultimately lose touch during the Tiananmen Square massacre of 1989. It was a raw and sensitive homage to the playwright's real life pen pal who went missing, and a timely tribute to the thousands of comrades who were injured or died fighting for their rights.

The show had a limited run in New York before playing, and friends and family came to support me during the first two weeks.

Winning and appearing in this role was important because it made me feel validated as an actor and as a person. I remember the day of the audition with utmost clarity: Young women lined up in typical fashion in the hallway of a West Village studio famous for acting, singing, and dance auditions.

Leaning against a wall or sitting on the floor were beautiful young women reading their sides and/or stretching their facial and body muscles into various states of contortion. I was always curious as to how they prepared for their auditions.

I wondered how much experience they'd had, what they'd appeared in, and with whom they studied. I lacked formal training, could not hold a tune or dance gracefully, and I was insecure, which is why I shied away from studying my lines in public, preferring instead to retreat to the bathroom to study.

Often while waiting for my turn, I would question why I showed up in the first place. "Who was I to think I could audition for a role like this?" "There are prettier girls here, and more talented ones." This was the type of self-talk I had grown accustomed to.

However, on this day, something unusual happened. The more I read the lines the more I felt a connection to the character, "Bibi."

Bibi reminded me of an older version of another character I had played in a 1968 production of "The King & I." Although the acting bug had already bitten me, it was there on the New York City Center stage, at age 10, that I had found my "voice."

I remember how my mom would escort my brother and me on the subway from Chinatown to West 57th Street, to this majestic building where everything seemed to just come alive. I don't know if it was my intuition or deja vu, but from the very first moment I stepped inside I was enveloped by a feeling of love and belonging.

I wanted to live there forever. The production – from start to finish – was transforming and transfixing me, and melding my character and me into one. Finally, I was in my element! Even the final death scene, *while the King lay dying every single night, I went to heaven.* The theatre was the only place in the world that offered a respite and a place to emote without fear of judgment, and to live completely in the moment.

Yet here I was 26 years later - a grown woman living in a child's mind, searching for the courage to audition and unaware that the experience would be forever life-changing. When my name was announced, I wandered into the room to face the expressionless casting directors, and prepared to fight with all my might.

As with all of the events in my life when placed in a spotlighted position, I became acutely aware that it wasn't just me and the honchos any more.

I could feel Bibi shoving aside my alter egos to allow for her energy to seep through. Her performance filled the room with a thick silence, then a palpable shift in energy … until slowly, I could feel her exit my body. Instinctively, I knew "we" had caught their attention, but there was still a catch. I had to read with the rest of the cast to ensure my "fit".

The callback was held on an unusually muggy summer day and I remember feeling very faint walking over to the repertory company from my apartment. I arrived pale and weak and barely able to stand, until a kindly man offered me a chair and a drink of water. Minutes later, a member of the staff came down to greet me and asked if I wanted to reschedule, but I knew that nothing in the world was going to stop me now that I had come this far!

I climbed the stairs to the second floor and there on a long communal table sat about a dozen people, and what surprised me was that I did not feel intimidated. Reading with them was surreal and when it was over, I knew by the glances being exchanged that I had earned the role!

During rehearsals I learned about staging, quickie wardrobe changes, and creative ways to adorn a dressing room. The only challenges that besieged me were finding inspiration in repetition, and mastering the art of emotional suppression. The former was easier, but for someone who is easily prone to crying, emotional suppression proved far more difficult.

I often looked to outward stimuli and inhabitations of Natalie Wood's Maria in "West Side Story," and sometimes I would anchor in to memories of "The King & I."

No death scene, however, could ever have prepared me for what was to happen next. In December of 1991, a month before she would turn 80, my beloved Poh Poh passed on. This was the first time I had ever lost anyone dear to me.

My mother and her siblings kept watch as everyone waited for Poh Poh's eldest to come home. I'll never forget the day I got the call. I was out doing what any ignorant, selfish young woman would do. I went shopping. Shopping – and shopping in excess – is, after all, denial's best escape mechanism.

People put their lives on hold while they are living. I never knew they could put their lives on hold while they were dying. The mind is a powerful thing, and love is a powerful life spring.

My grandma was my first role model. She came to this country at an early age and alongside her husband became a pillar of Chinatown's society in the early 1920's. When my grandpa died at the age of 55, Poh Poh found the strength to move on, raising four children on her own. Always the trendsetter, Poh Poh was the epitome of what it meant to be unstoppable. She had the combination of drive, command and indomitable spirit very few people possessed in her day.

On a night when I needed support the most, the very person I would turn to was gone from my life. I felt sure I would fall prey to histrionics or brain fog and honestly, I didn't give a damn. I was relieved that the producer let me off the hook and supported my decision not to perform the last show.

I struggled with twinges of guilt, and it wasn't until my mother uttered, "You have to perform the last show. Poh Poh was very proud of you," that I was able to muster the courage to go on. My Poh Poh was a warrior and my hero. How could I let her down?

On the final day of performance, I recall sitting lackluster and lifeless in the dressing room. The cast did not know what to say to me. No one spoke at all. I felt frozen in time and space. I thought about the irony of art imitating life, and life imitating art. I don't remember a thing from that performance and I'm sure there were lapses and missed cues, but when it came time for the monologue - I don't know if I was dreaming or if I blacked out but there I stood, looking out into the void again as I have for years, and suddenly I remembered a story Poh Poh had relayed to me.

I envisioned her as a child of about five, running and searching frantically for her family during a time of civil unrest. I envisioned her in a two-piece pink satin qipao, pigtails flapping in the wind and running… searching… screaming… "Mama?" "Baba?"

As I opened my mouth (presumably to speak) I could feel her blood coursing through my veins. I could feel her lifting me as she rose back up… running and screaming, searching and never giving up in her quest. There were so many things going through my mind, body, and soul and all I could think about was that while I was dying inside, my grandmother was in Heaven.

I was hypnotized by the imagery, so much so that I barely heard the sniffles in the remote distance, followed by applause. I knew in that instant what it meant to be strong and triumphant. And then, it dawned on me. Not once did I feel compelled to cry! Courage had replaced my tears, and seconds before the curtain fell I heard a warrior whisper, "It's going to be all right."

When I placed my heart on the stage that night, I was celebrating Poh Poh's life and joyful spirit, and the lessons I learned from her strength and character. She has taught me so much about having confidence, and I am grateful and blessed to have had the time I had with her, and to have witnessed the beacon of light that she was to so many. She stood for everything I believe in and every now and then, in the moments when I catch myself wavering or wallowing, she is there to guide me and remind me that the show always goes on.

America's Love Your Life coach, Caryn Chow, is a happiness expert and healer who has inspired audiences on how to achieve life transformation. One of her passions is coaching with public speaking, because "I get to watch my client transform before my eyes." When not blogging or writing her book, Caryn enjoys acting, performing, traveling, and yoga.

www.carynchow.com

PERSONAL GROWTH

The only journey is the one within.

– Rainer Maria Rilke

CHAPTER 23

CHEATING THE FUTURE YOU

BY STEVE GOODIER

Maybe you've had this experience. I recall one afternoon when I attended a parent-teacher conference for my second-grade son. We sat in the children's chairs. The seat was about a foot off the ground and certainly not made for adults. Those chairs were designed for little people. And as I sat uncomfortably waiting for the conference to begin, I had time to think about how much bigger I've gotten over the years. I clearly don't fit into the small furniture anymore.

We all grow. And, whether we are aware of it or not, we all change. We not only grow physically, we change in other ways. For instance, we grow in our roles. I occasionally asked my adolescent kids, "How do you think you're doing raising your parents?" I understood that I had to continually change my methods of parenting if I were to relate well to my children as they matured.

One mother told of how she changed as a parent. She mentioned that when her first baby coughed or sneezed, they'd practically rush her to the hospital. But Mom mellowed over the years. One day her youngest swallowed a dime. No hospital visits. No histrionics. She just said, "You know, don't you, that the dime will come out of your allowance?"

We grow in our roles. And we grow in other ways also. We grow mentally. I hope you are wiser and more knowledgeable today than you were in the past.

And we grow emotionally. Are you better at handling adversity today? Are you a kinder, more generous person? Do you find it easier to love and forgive? Dr. Karl Menninger said this about love and growth: "We do not fall in love, we grow in love and love grows in us." Is love growing in you?

We also have the chance to grow in another important way -- spiritually. I hope your spirituality is not the same as it was when you were a child. You

177

probably discovered that the spirituality that worked so well for you back then no longer satisfies.

Many children were taught to pray something like this: "Now I lay me down to sleep, I pray thee Lord my soul to keep. And if I die before I wake, I pray thee Lord my soul to take." (Actually, that prayer is a little brutal when you think about it, and I'm told that it originated from a time when plagues swept Europe and children feared that they indeed may not awaken from sleep.) But, if you're like most people, your spirituality matured as you grew up. A child may pray, "Give me…" or "Help me…" When she becomes an adult, she may find herself more often praying, "Use me…." or simply "Thank you."

We never stop growing and changing. We grow firmer or more flexible in our attitudes. We develop new skills and abilities. We grow in vision and we grow in confidence. We may also change in negative ways if we're not careful. We may grow more fearful, more cynical, or insensitive to others. We may even find ourselves becoming people we don't like very much. Life is all about growing and changing.

There are few exceptions to this rule. In fact, the only folks I know that never change reside in communities we call cemeteries.

One woman was shopping for Thanksgiving supper. None of the turkeys she found were large enough to feed her family. "Do these turkeys get any bigger?" she asked the young man stocking the shelves. "No, ma'am," he said. "They're all dead."

If we're dead, we won't grow. But if we're alive, we will. The only question is, will you decide how you want to grow? Will you decide to take responsibility for shaping your life? Because, if you don't make a decision about how you're going to grow, life will make it for you. If you're not in the process of becoming the person you want to be, you are in the process of becoming someone you had no intention of being.

I find one question that, if asked repeatedly, has an amazing power to put intentional growth on the fast track. This one question, more than anything else, can help you take control of how you will grow and change. The question is, "What would the person I want to become do in this situation?" That question alone will help you make different decisions, change the way you act and even change the way you think. That one question, asked regularly, may be the single most important way to take control of how you will grow in body, mind, emotions and spirit. Let me show you how it works.

What if you lost your job or suffered a serious financial setback? You might want to just give up. Instead, ask the question, "What would the person I want to become do in this situation?" Then decide to do it. You may not feel at all hopeful. You may even be afraid. But if the person you want to become is an optimistic and courageous person, you might decide not to react in fear. Instead, you might act as if you had no fear of failure and courageously put yourself out there for new employment opportunities. Or you may look at your job loss as an chance to go back to school instead of wasting time on regrets, depression, or fearful inaction.

Or how about this? Let's say you were betrayed or somehow deeply hurt by a trusted friend or relative. You may want to strike back in an equally hurtful way, or simply have nothing to do with them anymore. Instead, ask the question, "What would the person I want to become do in this situation?" Then act on that answer. You probably feel anger and more pain than you care to admit, but if the person you want to become is an emotionally strong individual, you might decide to act with strength, rather than licking your wounds. You might choose an appropriate way to confront that friend and tell her how you feel, talk the problem through, and even be ready to forgive if a valued relationship can be restored.

Asking yourself this question regularly and then acting on your answer will shape you bit by bit into a person you admire and respect. No situation is too big or too small. It works equally well with daily irritants and life's bigger challenges.

Take road rage. It is irritating to be honked at or cut off in traffic by an angry driver. You may find yourself reacting in a flash of temper. Next time that occurs, ask the question, "What would the person I want to become do in this situation?" Then choose, in that moment, a different way to respond. If the future you, the person you want to become, were abundantly patient and understanding, you might decide to laugh it off and use the opportunity to work on your sense of humor or to spend the next 15 minutes practicing peace of mind.

Or perhaps you are concerned about some of life's weightier problems, such as the plight of the poor. But the problems seem so overwhelming you feel stymied. As a result, you do little to help. Instead, ask the question, "What would the person I want to become do in this situation?" Then actually do it. If you imagine that the person you want to become is generous and engaged in social problems, you might find a local project and volunteer time and, if possible, money. You would figure out how to make volunteer service and generosity, or even advocacy for the poor, part of your increasingly engaged lifestyle.

I think George Bernard Shaw was right when he said, "Life isn't about finding yourself. Life is about creating yourself." Creating yourself may be the most vital and important job you do. It is the task of every day. And it is also an important gift you give yourself - the gift of creating the person you want to be.

Don't get me wrong. It's not that you're not wonderful now. You might be just the person you need to be in this moment. Enjoy yourself. Even celebrate yourself. After all, it took a lifetime to get where you are today! But remember...someone else is waiting ahead - a different version of you. And you have the opportunity to create that person, little by little, every day.

Steve Goodier is an ordained minister and author of several books. He writes a blog and syndicated newspaper column, publishes a weekly newsletter, and is featured regularly in the magazine CYACYL 24/Seven as well as personal growth websites. He believes that our lives can be lived fully and each of us can make a positive difference in our world.

www.LifeSupportSystem.com

PERSONAL SPACE

The light is what guides you home,
the warmth is what keeps you there.
– Ellie Rodriguez

CHAPTER 24

CALMING YOUR ENVIRONMENT

BY ROXANNE D'ANGELO

Everything in our world is made of energy and vibrating at different frequencies, including ourselves. Our material world naturally carries a dense low vibration. However, there are many natural elements readily available to us that hold a higher vibration, which can be incorporated immediately into our personal space, thereby creating an ongoing healing effect.

Our bodies are made up of an energetic system as well, mainly consisting of chakras and meridians. Our subtle bodies, when in a state of complete balance, carry a higher vibration than our material world while the opposite occurs when we are ill.

Let us take a look at the energy in our material world, the effects it can have on our bodies, and what we can do to shift the energy to create an ongoing healing environment.

FENG SHUI

Feng shui is an ancient Japanese art which creates harmony between people and their personal environment. Before applying any feng shui principles, it is important to address any dysfunctions within the space you are going to work on such as clearing clutter, organizing, and deep cleaning.

Once you have addressed these issues, you can move forward by taking inventory of your life and seeing what areas need improvement. Is it love, finances, career, health, or family? Are your creative juices blocked? Are your mentors showing up in your life to help guide you? Do others respect you?

Feng shui considers these areas of our lives and much more in order to create harmony. Applying feng shui principles helps us to manifest abundant health, wealth, and happiness through the flow of positive energy.

SOUND HEALING

According to Japanese researcher Dr. Masaru Emoto, our thoughts, words, and the music we listen to have the ability to affect water, including the 70 percent of water in our bodies. This happens through the transfer of vibrational frequencies.

Having thoughts of gratitude, speaking words of compassion, and listening to beautiful music and sound daily have a direct effect on our subtle bodies, helping to create a natural healing vessel.

Sound healing is being incorporated into mainstream medicine today. The use of Tibetan Singing Bowls is being used successfully in the recovery for cancer patients, as well as helping reduce anxiety and depression.

AROMA THERAPY

Most of us do not consider that the scent of our personal space could affect the well-being of our body, mind, and spirit. Well, surprisingly enough, it does. Our sense of smell affects the limbic system of our brain.

The limbic system is directly connected to those parts of the brain that control heart rate, blood pressure, breathing, memory, stress levels, and hormone balance.

Natural elements such as medical grade essential oils can have a profound physiological and psychological effect on your health. Anxiety, depression, fear, anger, joy, and happiness all emanate from the limbic regions of the brain.

If you desire a healthier body, mind, spirit, and personal environment, consider the use of medical grade essential oils on a daily basis.

CLEAR CLUTTER/ORGANIZE

Clutter carries a low dense vibration, which leaves an imprint on our subtle bodies. When our personal space is full of clutter it can leave us feeling, depressed, anxious, panicky, tired, and confused because of the overwhelming amount of low dense energy. Have you ever noticed that as soon as you begin to pick up things off the floor, the energy lifts? That is because you moved stagnant energy off the floor, allowing a flow of lighter energy to permeate that space. So you can begin to see how clearing clutter plays a very important role in raising your personal vibration.

Take a close look at all the items in your space. Evaluate each item to see how much it means to you. If there are items you have outgrown or don't cherish any longer, then perhaps it's time to let them go. Once this step is accomplished, what will be left are all the possessions that you love. Remember, our home is our sanctuary. It is truly amazing how much love our personal spaces can give back to us. And we already have most of the makings.

Once we have uncluttered, the next step is to begin organizing our space, which is crucial to energy flow. It also makes it much easier to find things, less confusing, allowing us to be more productive. When our space is organized, it resonates with our subtle bodies by raising our vibration.

DIRT

Did you know that dirt and dust carry a very low dense vibration? Well it does! You've heard the old saying, "Cleanliness is next to Godliness." Growing up in an Italian family, I sure learned a lot about this old adage at a very young age, perhaps when I was in the womb! We did spring cleaning, which is, cleaning the house from top to bottom and inside out, four times a year, with the seasonal changes.

I soon began to realize that spring time lasted all year! Actually back in the day, people from certain cultures had a yearly ritual which took place around the New Year. They did their form of spring cleaning to sweep away all the old negative energies out of their home, allowing new positive energy to flow in for the New Year! So keep in mind when we clean our space we are honoring our possessions, our selves, and raising the vibration of our personal space.

SPACE CLEARING

We don't realize how much energy affects our lives. Say someone has had an argument in your home. Did you know that the low energy from these angry words can affect your health? If done over and over, that negative energy can begin to take up residence in your home, and become part of your home's energy field, which can affect us on a chronic level.

Perhaps there is or was a lot of illness in your home. That low dense energy can affect everyone living in your home. How about when we move into a new home or apartment. The last occupant's energy becomes part of that space, which can have a direct effect on our wellbeing.

Space clearing clears out any leftover negative energies, and is replaced with positive loving energy, leaving the occupants of that space feeling lighter, relaxed, able to focus better, and more be creative. Often after a space clearing session, clients reported having better relationships with other members of the household.

ENERGY HEALING

When we integrate an energy healing modality such as Reiki, while raising the vibration of our personal space, we create a synergy of high vibration frequencies, allowing us to create abundance on all levels of life.

The purpose of Reiki is to cleanse, balance, and heal all of our chakras, allowing natural healing to occur. Reiki is a peaceful healing modality, which reconnects us to Divine Love. Once we fill our lives inside and out with this pure love, we are able to handle our daily stresses with more ease and confidence.

TIPS FOR CLEARING NEGATIVE ENERGY FROM YOUR PERSONAL SPACE

Music: Playing beautiful music daily creates positive energy and can help ease stress and depression

Aroma: Diffuse therapeutic grade essential oils to shift energy of your space creating a healing atmosphere

Clear Clutter: Clearing clutter will help raise the energy of your space and leave you feeling energized

Organize: Keeping our homes well organized allows energy to flow freely and keep us focused

Keep It Clean: "Cleanliness is next to Godliness" Cleaning allows the light to shine in on our homes and our hearts

Open Windows: Allow fresh air in daily, even if for only a few minutes to release any negative energy and leave us feeling renewed

Wind Sensitive Objects: Simple wind chimes can create a feeling of overall peace, providing the chimes are not in a direct area where too much wind may pass through

Water Fountains: Just listening to the sound of a gentle water fall in a quiet corner of your favorite room can leave you feeling relaxed, at peace, and allow your creative juices to flow

Lighting: Having proper lighting in any room can change the energy instantly, giving us a new perspective of the area

Words: Use beautiful words daily to create a gravitational force, attracting likeness into our lives, like Joy and Love

Thoughts: Coming from a place of gratitude and compassion can change our overall life experiences to that of Happiness

Roxanne D'Angelo works as an integrative medicine healing practitioner, integrating multiple healing modalities into her practice. She is an intuitive feng shui and space clearing consultant, sound healing and crystal practitioner, and essential oil consultant. Roxanne is certified as a Reiki and Arch Master/Teacher.

www.crystalclearenergies.com

PURPOSE

When you walk in purpose,
you collide with destiny.
– Ralph Buchanan

CHAPTER 25

PURPOSE: DISCOVER YOURS – YOU'RE WORTH IT!

BY DENISE HANSARD

What's your passion? What's your purpose? Do you know?

If you bought this book looking for either of these, guess what? *Passion* is easy. Yes, passion is easy. Yet it is never *about* the passion – shoes, chocolate, tequila – and other things that bring you moments of pleasure. It's about *meaning* – having a true understanding of who you are in the world and what you're here to do, and then using this sense of yourself as the foundation for how you live your life.

Chances are, to the outside world, there is nothing wrong with your life. You have a good job. You have a good relationship. You have good health. But did you wake up this morning (or any morning, for that matter) asking yourself, "Is there something more?"

Yes, there is! And it lies in your purpose.

PURPOSE IS WORTH IT

Searching for your purpose in life could look like hard work. Some of this may be because you keep digging into your past not seeming to find "it" – whatever "it" is. You just keep asking yourself, "Isn't there *more?*"

I am here to tell you, "Yes, there is! And that's your purpose!" Discovering it is worth your effort! When you are aligned with your purpose, I promise you, you will never again feel this lack.

So, are you ready to learn more about finding your purpose? If so, I'm thrilled to support you.

AN ARCHITECT

Why can I help you? I have a master's degree in counseling. This means I used to dig into people's pasts just like an *archeologist*. Here's the irony. No matter how hard I dug with the people I worked with, this didn't seem to do anything except keep them in the past. Today, my clients get results because I am an *architect*—building the foundation that will support living life as they are meant to.

Everyone has a purpose. Everyone is here for a reason. Your job is probably OK, yet you feel as if you have been pigeon holed, undervalued, and always overlooked for that next promotion. Your relationship is OK, yet you want more passion, spontaneity, and more of what it used to be when you first fell in love. Your health is OK, yet it is easy to turn off the morning alarm, rationalizing that you will go to exercise class tomorrow morning.

I'm going to share with you not only how to stop playing *small* in your life, but how to *transform* it – into the one you were *meant* to live.

MAKE A CLEAR TRANSFORMATION

I have found—for myself and my clients—that there are five steps to transforming a life. To make these easy to remember and follow, I use the word "CLEAR."

C – Choice. Recognize that everything in life is a choice. Every thought you have; every action you take; every involuntary reaction you make is a choice. We have become conditioned to think that sometimes we don't have choices. That is also a choice—to be a victim. Everything in life is a choice, and we get to make it!

L – Language. How we express our thoughts when we speak—to ourselves and others—comes from our choices. We learn patterns of language that keep us victimized or help us to grow into victors! A good example is the word "but." It has become overused and a "filler word" in our language. Yet, its meaning is extremely powerful. Everything you state *after* this word negates everything you said *before* it!

Here's an example: "I love you but I don't like what you did." The first part—stating you love someone—is totally wiped away with that three-letter word! "But" stops most of us from living our lives to the fullest. We allow it to put the brakes on what we really want. My best advice is to get off your "but" altogether! Instead, put a period at the end and start a new sentence. Now we have: "I love you. I don't like what you did." This totally changes the emotions behind what is being said. Use positive language in everything you say.

E – Energized. When our words are positive, they energize us to begin the process toward change, toward transformation. You just saw how our words have power. They can change relationships with ourselves and with others. Remember: what we say to ourselves (internal trash talk: "I can't," "what makes me think it will work this time," etc.) is usually how we live our life. This always moves us in the direction of "not good enough" behaviors. Turn off the volume on that negative voice inside your head. Get energy from using positive words. You'll be amazed at how this one step improves your life.

A – Actions. Using those affirming words has a direct and powerful impact on our actions. Try it out right now! Think of an issue or opportunity that's confronting you. As you speak to yourself and others about it, choose "why not" instead of "why;" "I choose" instead of "I can't;" "I am" instead of "I want, hope, wish." This predisposes you to take action with more confidence and assurance, rather than from a place of uncertainty, doubt and despair. Claim your power!

R – Results. Your results become more attuned to the idea to "live like you were meant to." When you make defined choices, decisions become clear and easier to make. There is less stress because you are focused on the *results* rather than letting *circumstances* to rule your life. If you don't like the results in your life, then go back to your choices and change them—as this changes your life!

Seems simple, doesn't it? Then why aren't you further along in knowing your purpose in life? Why do you feel stuck?

FEAR USUALLY STOPS US – AND HOW TO GET STARTED AGAIN

Fear will always be with you. It's what you *do* with your fear that allows you to move out of your "stuckness" or keeps you right where you are. Choosing to see fear as a *friend* and not your constant enemy is a freeing alternative!

Opportunities come into your life every day. Someone may talk to you about a new job or a seminar she wants you to attend. Or you may have a chance to do something you truly love: start a business, have the wonderful relationship you are looking for, or move up that career ladder and make more money than you have ever have. When these opportunities come, you have three choices:

• Say "yes" and step into your growth

• Say "no" and own this choice—even if you might regret it later

• Make no choice whatsoever, letting the opportunity pass you by—and then looking back and making excuses for why you didn't make a decision

In reality, there are really only *two* choices you can make: yes or no. Allowing chances to slip away due to fear, lack of clarity, or just convincing yourself that you don't have the time, money, or education is *not* a choice. It's just your fear getting in the way and blinding you to better outcomes.

Accept that you have fear in your life. Then refuse to see it as debilitating. Instead, it's an opportunity to grow! This is the first step toward changing your life. There are more steps—and, the good news is *you don't have to do it alone.*

No one became a world-class athlete by herself. The same is true for having a world-class life. Aligning yourself with a coach to help with your personal transformation is one way to make this happen. Deciding to invest in you now is the most important step you can take now! Go out and get that *more* in your life!

Denise Hansard, a Southern girl who loves to tell stories, made a choice to free herself from her past stories, which no longer define her. With her Masters in Counseling, life coach certification, and 20 years of corporate work, Denise uses her passion for helping people become their best selves.

www.denisehansard.com

RELATIONSHIPS

Relationship is an art. The dream that two people create is more difficult to master than one.

– Don Miguel Ruiz

CHAPTER 26

SEVEN WAYS TO SAVE A STRUGGLING RELATIONSHIP

BY CARMEN HARRA, Ph.D., AND ALEXANDRA HARRA

After her husband died, I watched my 80-year-old next door neighbor live out halfhearted days in quiet sobs. During one of my visits to her home, she confessed that she spent equal parts of her marriage frustrated as she did happy. "There were times when I wanted to pack my things and just leave him," she said as her eyes swelled with new tears, "but I never did."

My neighbor braved the typical (sometimes extreme) ups and downs of a relationship for a full 60 years. Her pride was not in that she had found a relationship, but in that she had kept it for so long. And the only secret to an everlasting marriage, she revealed, was this: "Hold your spouse closer to your heart than you hold your own ego."

Nowadays, we believe that people are *exchangeable*. Quick are we to think, "He's no good, I'll dump him and find someone else." And quicker are we to find a new lover who displays the exact same - if not worse - tendencies as the one we just left.

We are taught to be independent, and this is an incredible discipline; we are self-made and self-sustainable. But taken to the extreme, this attitude is guaranteed to interfere in our relationships. No one can be exchanged for anyone else. Your partner is not a pair of pants you picked up at Macy's. Your partner was placed in your life for a greater reason in divine timing. He or she is a human being brimming with flaws and awful failings, but also abounding with potential integrity.

Beware of abandoning someone just because they require a bit of inner repair work. You do, too. This is not to say that you should ever settle for an unhealthy situation, but a successful relationship entails honest work and the payoff can be extraordinarily rewarding in terms of not just finding, but keeping, long-term love.

If you believe you can sift through people until you find the perfect package, you will remain highly disappointed throughout your relationships. You may find someone different, perhaps a bit better, but who will still need "fixing." We enter a new relationship bearing the open wounds of our former experiences, hungry for healing and emotional nourishment from our partner. And each person we encounter will test our capacity for sacrifice, compromise, patience, and tolerance. A real relationship that endures through time is one in which you have poured forth more love and understanding than you ever thought possible of you.

It's admirable to believe in the unique power of your relationship, and even wiser to realize that no, you won't magically stumble upon a fairytale romance. If you currently find yourself in a relationship that's weak, broken, or on the brink of collapse, but that you believe deserves your effort, don't give up. Consider these seven ways to save your struggling relationship:

1. Re-evaluate the reasons you are together. Go back to the beginning. Ask yourself: What drew me to this person to begin with? What qualities did they possess that I found valuable? What made them so amazing? And are they still? Reevaluating the reasons you came together reminds you of the reasons to stay together, and this strengthens your already-existing foundation. Ask your partner what they love and don't love about you; be open to constructive criticism and self-improvement.

2. Communicate. There is a right way and a wrong way to communicate. The right way is asking your partner a relevant question, listening to their response, then offering your opinion. The wrong way is overwhelming your partner with your irritations and worries as soon as they walk in from a particularly long workday. Practice effective speech by engaging your loved one in a conversation of their interest. Ask questions that matter to them; people open up when you inquire about their day, an important project, their feelings, etc. Once you've listened to what they have to say, offer your side of the story. Stay away from heavy conversations in stressful times, and especially in the heat of emotion. Calm down, then approach the topic again. Don't just sound off with your concerns; delve to the core of the matter by drawing your partner into the dialogue first.

3. Do something special together. Perhaps you two have a favorite restaurant you haven't visited in ages, or you can return to the place where you first fell in love? Being in a physical space where you have powerful memories of strong attachment can reignite passion. Or, you can try something you've never tried before. The excitement of something new produces serotonin and dopamine in our brains. It doesn't have to be something extraordinary; even sitting on a park bench watching the children play as you hold hands can be magical if love exists. The important thing is that you stop talking about taking that vacation, or trying that new spot, and follow through on your intention to reconnect together.

4. Cut out external influences. Often it is outside voices that seep into our private relationships and brew toxicity. Understand who's playing a less-than-positive role in your relationship and commit to keeping that person's energy out! Keep your relationship as private as possible and divulge as few details as you can. Don't automatically admit your love woes to others. Chances are they don't hold the answers to your problems. Open up the gateways of communication instead and confess your concerns to your partner.

5. Forgive each other. To forgive is to detach – from the bitterness, anger, and animosity holding you back from progress with your partner. Forgo the negative emotions keeping you from true forgiveness. Remind yourself that whatever happened, happened, and that there is no reason to drag the past into your future. Lingering on hurtful memories only perpetuates them. Be mindful that forgiveness is a process, not a result, so perform small, daily acts that are reflective of your intent to pardon.

6. Come clean about one thing. We all hold a few secrets that would deeply hurt others if they found out. This is normal. Certain things should simply be kept to ourselves. But honesty can trigger wonders in your partner's opinion of you. Admitting one secret or mistake to your partner may make them want to open up, too.

7. Set boundaries with each other. And keep your word! If you set a rule for your partner, set a similar one for yourself as well. This means that if your partner promises not to stay out late on a Saturday, you should abide by the same principle. A relationship is a two-way street. Tell your partner honestly what you would like them to do (or not do), then be prepared to accept the boundaries they set for you, too. Maintaining a relationship within comfortable bounds avoids arguments, explosions, and setbacks. It aids mutual growth if both partners are respectful toward the other's wishes. It also promotes a sense of security and trust that each is acting in good faith.

While we should never remain in a relationship that jeopardizes our well-being, all relationships will require our earnest effort and compliance with our partner's needs. Not giving up on someone and trying our very best to make it work are honorable tasks to undertake. Use my seven ways to save your struggling relationship and reap the benefits of an unbreakable loving bond.

Carmen Harra, Ph.D., is an internationally acclaimed intuitive psychologist, author, relationship expert, spiritual teacher, and karmic counselor. Carmen has appeared in broadcast media and has been featured in numerous publications such as New York Times, New York Post, New York Daily News, *among others. She is the author of the international best-seller,* Everyday Karma, *and her seventh book,* The Karma Queens' Guide to Relationships. *Carmen hosts her own radio show on titled Miracle Guidance for Everyday Life.*

Alexandra Harra is a professional writer, certified life coach, cover model, Huffington Post *contributor, and author of the book* The Karma Queens' Guide to Relationships. *Alexandra holds degrees in Creative Writing and Classics and is trilingual, speaking English, Romanian, and Spanish fluently. She has appeared on a multitude of TV shows and in publications in Europe.*

www.CarmenHarra.com
www.AlexandraHarra.com

RESILENCY

Man never made any material as
resilient as the human spirit.
– Bernard Williams

CHAPTER 27

I WILL NOT LAY DOWN AND DIE!

BY SHANNON HROBAK SENNEFELDER

It has been over 20 years since I left a violent abusive relationship that left me ready to give up; to just lay down and die. I fell in love with someone who was violent and abusive. I spent several years fearing him to the point of giving up my will to live. It has taken me countless years, endless prayers, wishful demands to God and the universe, and a whole lot of self-excavation to create a new normal. The person who abused me has passed away. It is apparent that he is no longer a "threat." Yet, years later, I am still living with and managing my own PTSD.

Fast forward to my life now. I've worked tirelessly to manage fears and unsettling and false beliefs about my own safety. My husband and I have worked together to create a safe, loving home. It has become my sanctuary. Even my home office is Zen. In my career, I often travel to speak and lead workshops and retreats. I spend time in hotels, airports among strangers, in high energy places, so I especially look forward to coming home to my family and my sanctuary, affectionately referred to as "my soft place to land."

Recently, our local power company began construction on a new substation. The location is just beyond our property line, adjacent to my office window. My daily ritual normally begins with yoga and meditation. When I'm home it's done either in my office or on my back deck.

For days, I've been walking around my home grumbling and snarling with frustration. I've been complaining to my husband that *they* have no right to invade *my* privacy. Why must they build so close to *our* home? The arrival of these uninvited intruders has resulted in my home no longer feeling "safe" for me. It took me a while to arrive at this revelation.

Yesterday, in the midst of one of my rants, I found myself screaming and crying simultaneously, while pacing around my house. "I am so mad! I am so mad!" I shouted, waving my fists in the air. Somehow, I heard my phone ring, saw it was my business partner and dearest friend, Carle. I picked up and jumped right in, "I'm so glad you called! I AM SO MAD! I AM FURIOUS THAT THESE %@#@%$^ men are making so much noise, building this damn building near my property!"

Carle is smart enough and patient enough to know to sit back and ride the crazy train rant when I get like this. He knows not to rush me to a solution; rather, he lets me discover it on my own through talking it out- or in this case, screaming, pacing, and waving my fists.

It wasn't long before his calm voice, accurate questions, and my willingness to trust his help, brought me to my truth. I wasn't mad at these men for doing their job. I wasn't even mad at myself for getting so angry.

My truth is that I was scared and felt completely vulnerable, just like I felt years ago. I was terrified that my safe place no longer felt safe. I was experiencing that vulnerable, helpless feeling that something was about to happen *to* me, and I couldn't do a damn thing to stop it.

Do you recall the music from *Jaws*? The deep resonating sounds that quicken as the danger approaches? The feeling that you get being fully aware that someone is about to get eaten? That is how I can describe the unsettling fear the consumes my body when I don't feel safe. And in one moment of clarity, I was able to say out loud, "Oh my gosh, I'm not angry. I am scared. I feel vulnerable and afraid. Just like I did years ago."

Now, I am also a very rational person, or at least I think I can be at times. Logically, I know that these men are not out to hurt me. Logically, I know that my abuser isn't going to try to break in. He is not even alive. Logically, I know that I am safe at home with two dogs that bark loudly, guns and ammunition to protect me if ever needed. I am safe. But that's the real down and dirty, ugly part of what PTSD does to a person. It takes the logical, realistic facts and suffocates them with fear, insecurities and irrational thoughts.

One of the key components to being able to find the source of my struggle is to be very aware of my own physiology and how accurate my body is at keeping me informed.

For example, I hold my tension in my shoulders first, then my neck. During my rant to Carle, my shoulders were so tight, I felt like they were at my ears. My neck was stiff. The moment I said aloud, "I'm not angry. I am scared," my shoulders fell. I could feel the tension release from my straining neck. My body was telling me, "Yes, that is your truth!" And I listened. Once I said out loud that I was no longer angry, I felt a calming peace wash over me. It reminded me of the warm ocean waves in Hawaii where I spent time with my girlfriends. I felt the warmth of peace and the beginning of feeling safe again. In that moment when I said out loud, "I'm not angry. I am scared," I named the beast. Immediately, it began to shrink.

When my husband came home, I explained it to him. I wasn't mad at these guys, I was afraid. My husband is a saint. He knows me so well and is always willing to support me. I knew exactly what to ask for.

I asked him to remind me that I am safe. I asked him to say out loud that he was there to help me and protect me. And I even asked him to beat up all of those guys, if they came near me, or our home, which made me laugh. The next morning, he said there was a problem with beating up those guys. He told me that the front license plate on one of their trucks had "Poppy" on it. What I haven't mentioned is that my Dad passed away two years ago. I miss him terribly and often find myself talking to him. I believe that he was talking to *me* that morning. Keith and I laughed that Poppy was probably at the job site bent over, digging a trench because my Dad lived and loved to work. Soon, I was laughing heartily. It took me a few hours, but eventually, I opened my windows again. By that afternoon, I had both front and back doors unlocked, and stepped outside for some fresh air. It took me some time, but I worked through it. I used the same resources that I teach to women every day.

I asked for help from people I trust. I listened to my body.

I work with women who struggle daily with fears, low self-esteem, self-worth. I also witness these same women work relentlessly to rediscover their worth and value and as cliche as it sounds; begin to believe three words that change the course of their future. "I AM ENOUGH."

Ahhh, can you feel the depth and breadth of those words? Do you wish and want to believe them? Even for a second? For a day? How about for the rest of your days?

It is possible. And you are well on your way.

Here's what else is possible. And if necessary, I will urge you to read these next several sentences as many times as necessary; until you are nodding along with me.

Read this out loud.

I believe that as long as there is breath in me, that I can change the course of my life. I have the power within me to do this. I have an abundance of resources, even if I cannot see them yet. I have around me, and within reach, powerful women who have been "there" just like me. They know me, and love me for who I am.

They will not judge me, or dismiss me. They are willing to stand with me and work with me so that I can stand up again. I am ready. I can do this. I am surrounded by hope. I am surrounded by love. I am surrounded by powerful women. I am worthy of this great life. I am worthy of living. I am worthy of being loved. I am worthy of being alive. I am enough.

I AM ENOUGH!

How do you feel now? Do you feel good? Then try these strategies to feel better! Still feel bad? Then try these to feel good!

1. Go outside. I don't care if it's too cold or too warm where you are. Go! Take your book with you! Once you're outside, take a deep breath. Do this three times. When you increase the oxygen flow in your body, it fires off neurotransmitters that help you to think and feel better. Seriously. Google it - "Brains and Behavior."

2. Contact someone you love - right now. I know you have your smarty-phone in your pocket. Get it out and text or Facebook one of your friends you care about right now. Here is the message. "YOU ARE ENOUGH." When we give, we get. It's inevitable. When we help others feel good; it helps us to feel good. Its the *Law of Attraction*.

3. Use that smarty-phone and google this: "Women's Resiliency Workshops" There are hundreds in the U.S. alone. Find one that is close to you. Contact them. Ask questions. Take that awesome woman you sent the message to

and invite her for coffee. Talk about your hopes and dreams. Laugh again. I dare you.

And if you get stuck, which we all do, go back to the previous paragraph and read it again. The truth is, changing the course of your life doesn't have to be hard! It does however require you to do one thing. Choose.

If you did any one of those three things above, you're further than you were before. This is a mantra that I heard at one of the many women's groups I attend, "Do the next right thing." That's it. Just one. And then, do it again. And again. You are worth it! Be Well. I AM.

Shannon Hrobak Sennefelder is the president and founder of White Swans Consulting, LLC, and lead facilitator of Love Your Outstanding Life, a division of WSC. She is an outstanding facilitator, resiliency expert, and keynote speaker for a variety of clients. Shannon is recognized for her energetic style and clear communication skills.

www.whiteswansconsulting.com

SELF IMAGE

Most of the shadows of this life are caused
by standing in one's own sunshine.

– Ralph Waldo Emerson

CHAPTER 28

YOUR GENIUS LIES WITHIN IF YOU HAVE THE COURAGE TO CLAIM IT AND IT ALL STARTS WITH SELF-IMAGE

BY MICHELLE WELCH

Until you begin the process of shifting your faulty beliefs, you won't be able to begin the process of tapping into your genius. Your genius is simply those attributes that either come naturally to you, skills you've mastered through repetition, or those passions you engage in where you lose track of all time.

Oftentimes we are unable to get clear on what our genius is because we have certain conflicting and self-induced limiting beliefs on how we should and shouldn't be in the world. Henry Ford once said, "Whether you think you can, or you think you can't you're right." Your self-image determines what you think you can or cannot do; and your beliefs ultimately dictate your actions.

You can liken your self-image to a blueprint, in this case a mental blueprint. A blueprint is simply a design plan. You can either design your self-image to be one that empowers you and tells you that anything is possible, or one that limits you, tells you what you can't do, and is filled with negativity and unproductive thoughts about yourself.

If I were to ask, "Who are you?," I am sure you could come up with a long list of ways to describe yourself: mom, female, male, business owner, procrastinator, someone who's tardy and so forth. Our self-image has been built up based on our past experiences, our beliefs which have been handed down to us by our caregivers, peers, and authority figures, how they react to us, and what we've told ourselves.

213

Our self-image is initially formed at the subconscious level mostly before the age of seven. By the age of seven, a child begins to move from an unconscious way of thinking to a conscious one. The images we've created become our truth and we act in accordance with that inherited truth, until we gather evidence to the contrary.

If your caregiver told you over and over when you were a child that you were stupid and wouldn't amount to anything, then that's the image you would have created of yourself until you consciously and actively began to change that self-image. Likewise, if he or she expressed to you that you were smart and beautiful, this would have created a totally different self-image.

Imagine in your mind for a moment a box, and within that box is a smaller box called your Self-Image. This self-image has preset beliefs and conditioned responses, including limiting beliefs passed down to you from those who had influenced you throughout your life. However, as you begin to actively change those limiting beliefs and take on new, more productive and empowering beliefs, that box gets bigger and bigger until it reaches the outside box where your full potential resides.

The question then remains, "How do you change your self-image?" It's a two-step process. The first step is to begin to explore what you think about yoursel for believe others think about you. Second, begin to fill your mind with new empowering thoughts and do this to such an extreme that your new beliefs overshadow your limiting and unproductive beliefs about yourself. It's going to take quite a bit of effort on your part, tuning into those internal conversations, then actively participating in changing your old beliefs and conversations.

In the beginning, you may come up against difficulty in believing these newly acquired beliefs. In his book *Psycho Cybernetics*, Maxwell Maltz stated, "Human beings always act and feel and perform in accordance with what they imagine to be true about themselves and their environment." But here's what's really interesting. The nervous system cannot tell the difference between an imagined experience and a "real" one. It reacts appropriately to what you think or imagine to be true. Therefore, by simply acting "as if" those new beliefs were true, you can begin the process of altering your self-image, until the new belief is implanted into your subconscious mind.

If you want to live your life by design, you need to bump up your self-image so it's congruent and aligned with your wants and desires. It's also important to develop a self-image that you believe in, that is open to creativity and full self-expression, and one that is built on honesty with what you can and cannot do that is, getting crystal clear on your actual strengths and weaknesses. Can you see how having a limiting or skewed self-image deters you from reaching your fullest potential and connecting to that genius that resides in you?

Your mind, much like your body, works on keeping homeostasis. Anytime if feels like it's going off track, it is going to kick in your automatic programming which comes from your subconscious belief system to put you back in line. That's its job. It is designed to keep you safe. Whether or not you consciously feel that all is safe is irrelevant. Your subconscious mind controls 95% of your daily actions. However, not all hope is lost.

What you see, hear, or experience repeatedly and with intensity is what begins to alter your self-image. This is great news because you know that you don't have to be a victim of your self-induced limiting beliefs and habits. You have the power to change.

By incorporating small, incremental daily actions and conversations, you can begin the process of altering your self-image into one that empowers you. As you begin to experience more and more success, your self-image slowly begins to change with it to align itself with your new way of being. The core message is that new experiences, in particular ones of success, is what begins to change your self-image.

The best way to begin to determine the characteristics of your self-image is to see what comes up for you when you say "I am." Your "I am" has been a way for you to identify yourself to yourself and to the world all throughout your life. It communicates to you, and others, what you can and cannot do, what you like or dislike, and who you are in reference to others, amongst other things. "I am" can be a powerful tool to help build up your self-image or diminish it.

Another way to determine the characteristics of your self-image is to explore where your beliefs came from. Think of yourself as Magnum, P.I. as you begin the investigative process of determining where your beliefs originated from. Beliefs are simply thoughts repeated over and over until they become recorded at the subconscious level. As you go through the process of sorting through your belief system, ask yourself one simple question: "Is this the truth?"

The genius lies within you, should you have the courage to claim it. Courage is not some esoteric quality, but rather a choice. You have in you access to all things possible. You are capable of reaching your fullest potential by accessing and expressing your genius. The key to this fullest self-expression is understanding and maximizing your self-image... and it always starts from within.

Michele Welch is a Business and Personal Growth Catalyst and founder of TheEdgeCode. com site dedicated to helping entrepreneurs create a profitable business and inspired life. She specializes in helping business owners troubleshoot and implement marketing strategies, in some cases increasing revenues by over 300 percent.

www.TheEdgeCode.com

SUCCESS

Don't aim for success if you want it; just do what
you love and believe in, and it will come naturally.

– David Frost

CHAPTER 29

TEN RULES FOR CAREER AND LIFE SUCCESS

BY AMY REECE CONNELLY

Some time ago, just before a book I had co-authored with a colleague was published, I was asked to speak about success with a group of high school sophomores from my hometown who were being honored for their scholastic achievement. These are the Top Ten Rules for Success I shared with them:

10. Control the voices inside your head. There's a theory that you are most like the four or five people with whom you spend the most time.

Dave Ramsey, a nationally-known money expert, says that "Five years from now you will be the same person you are today except for the books you read and the people you meet."

What are YOU reading? Or watching on television? Or listening to on your iPhone? Who are you hanging out with? You get to choose your influences. Are they leading you down the road to success?

9. Never stop learning. Your formal education will end, but there are always opportunities to learn new things. They don't have to be lofty. Learn how to iron a shirt properly. Or how to plant tomatoes. In fact, DO NOT move away from home without knowing how to change a tire, do your laundry, sew on a button, and cook at least three things that don't involve the use of a microwave oven or ramen noodles.

Try something new. You will never know if you like something until you've tried it. It may even lead you to a career you've never considered.

8. Look both ways before crossing the street. In other words, be aware of your surroundings and what's going on in the world. Challenge what you think you know. Actively seek opinions different from yours. Question both authority and the status quo. What's right isn't always what's popular. Centuries ago, everyone believed the world was flat.

Thirty years ago, it snowed for half an hour in the Sahara Desert, and experts thought we were headed for a new ice age. I suppose they could be wrong about global warming.

7. Use your resources wisely. According to TotalBankruptcy.com, "people in their early twenties... are among the fastest growing group of bankruptcy filers." This report further states that "the average college student graduates with between $3000 and $4000 in credit card debt." That doesn't include student loans they may have picked up along the way.

Carrying a high debt load can affect your ability to pursue your goals, especially if you have to quit school to pay your debts. Debt can affect what kind of a job you can get, what kind of car you drive, and whether you can afford to purchase a home.

If you can learn how to manage your time and make your money work for you, you will create wonderful long-term opportunities for yourself.

6. Set goals. I like to-do lists. In fact, I'm one of those people who will add something I just did to my list so I can have the pleasure of crossing it off.

It's important to have some goals that you can reach no matter where you are in life. Some time ago, when I was a stay-at-home Mom with two babies in diapers, I resolved never to run out of bathroom tissue. That goal got me through some tough months. It was tangible and measurable, and although the bigger goal was to raise respectable, responsible adults, in the short-term, I could see I was making progress.

Mix it up a little bit. Give yourself a few easy targets, but make sure there are a few things on your list that will force you to stretch, as well.

5a. Don't be afraid to make mistakes. Don't fear failure. Some of the greatest inventions occurred only after multiple misfires. A friend of mine who works for Eli Lilly told me that employees there are encouraged to "make mistakes FAST," as the quicker they find out what DOESN'T work, the quicker they can find the real solutions.

I knew people in both high school and college who didn't take a class in which they had some interest—and at which they might have excelled--because it might have negatively affected their grade point average.

You may learn more from your failures than from your successes. You will definitely learn what you are made of and what you can overcome.

5b. But avoid making stupid mistakes. Sadly, some of my classmates are no longer with us. One was killed trying to beat a train across the tracks. Another self-medicated with chemical substances that eventually destroyed her heart.

This is the stuff that scares Moms. Every day the news is filled with stories of young people who got behind the wheel of a car after drinking, or met up with a stranger they found on the Internet, or ended up in the wrong place at the wrong time with the wrong "friends." Life paths change with unplanned pregnancies; some lives end with sexually-transmitted diseases.

Consider the long-term consequences of your actions and inactions, and master the complementary arts of patience and delayed gratification.

4. Don't work for money. Of course, you should earn what you're worth. That's not my point here.

The toughest client I ever coached had made every choice in his life based on how much money he could make. He chose his academic course of study based, not on his interests and skills, but on income potential. This way of thinking had become so ingrained for him that he couldn't even identify anything that he liked to do when I asked him—other than make money. The problem was, he wasn't making any money. He hated his job. He hated his life. And he was beating himself up because he wasn't earning $500,000 a year.

If you choose a career based solely on income potential, you will EARN every dime. One of the secrets to success is choosing a career based on something you like to do. If you like it, you'll enjoy practicing the skills necessary to do it well. And when you do it well, you'll be successful. Do what you love, and it will never feel like work.

3. Acknowledge those who have helped you along the way. You didn't get here by yourself. Everyone who is honored by others today has at least one adult who took an interest in them and encouraged success. It's probably a parent or a grandparent. Or an aunt or uncle. Or a neighbor. A youth minister. A teacher. If you're lucky, you may have all of those. Recognize their sacrifices and thank them whenever you get a chance.

2. Choose to be a person of integrity. We all know "honor" students, but "HONOR" is so much more than just earning good grades. Webster defines honor as "respectful regard." Intelligence is not a necessary ingredient to become honorable. We are all like tea bags. We show our true character when we get into hot water. And you WILL get into hot water.

Keep your word. Admit your mistakes. Hold yourself accountable to yourself and others. Be a friend. And, as Gandhi said, "Be the change you want to see in the world."

FINALLY...

1. Don't take yourself too seriously. Throughout your life, you will be asked to make decisions that will be presented as "crucial to your future." What college are you going to attend? What major area of study are you going to pursue?

Getting into a great college and pursuing the major of your choice are important. But even more important is what you do with the opportunities that are presented to you.

There are a lot of career choices that have emerged over the last 30 years that didn't exist when I was in high school. Much of the work I do now has been made possible by technologies that were in their infancy just fifteen years ago. No doubt, there will be opportunities 30 years from now that have yet to be considered.

You are going to hear over the next several years that you are the future of the world. You are. But you don't have to take the reins tomorrow. Even when it is time for your generation to take over, you will not have the entire weight of the planet on your shoulders. There are just under seven billion of us who can share the load.

Thirty years will pass by quickly. You'll have lots of challenges that none of us can predict today. There will be good days and bad, the stock market will be up and down, and the tug of war between political ideologies will, no doubt, continue. But, you get to define what success is for you. Successful people are not always famous. They are not always wealthy.

I do believe, though, that happiness is a necessary element of success.

So, keep learning, keep laughing, and moisturize daily—because if you do it right, your laugh lines will be a measure of your success.

Amy Reece Connelly manages Corporate Communications and Training for REA, a NJ-based corporation specializing in international career transitions. She also is founder and principal of Connelly & Associates, Inc., where she provides career coaching for high school students, mid-life career changers, and veterans returning to civilian employment.

www.r-e-a.com
www.connellycareers.com

TRANSFORMATION

When I stand before God at the end of my life, I would hope that I would not have a single bit of talent left and could say, "I used everything you gave me."

– Erma Bombeck

CHAPTER 30

HOW TO TRANSFORM YOUR LIFE

BY MARY BATTAGLIA

Many people walk through life feeling that something is missing; that they are forced into the existence they lead. They follow a formula that society and their upbringing creates and live that way without questioning it. They make conscious choices to stay stuck because of fears and limiting beliefs. They remain in a rut or a bad relationship because it feels safe to stay in a familiar cocoon.

Sometimes there is a stirring of discontent or anger that leads to an awakening and a rejection of the way things are. Other times a jolt in life spurs change – a death in the family, job loss, or a relationship issue wakes them up to the realization that transformation needs to occur.

Transformation is about making changes in life. It may not seem easy at first to forge ahead on an uphill road not knowing the destination, but it is worth it when you reach the top and get to the place where you are meant to be in life. It is beautiful.

To be able to transform one must look within and ask questions. Am I happy? Am I still in love? Am I doing what I am meant to do? Why am I afraid? See what answers come out of this to determine what is lacking.

Just like in the spring when a cherry blossom tree comes alive, transformation is a gradual process. The branches go from being bare, to buds emerging, and soon flowers appear. The energy of the tree changes after the transformation. It attracts new and positive energy around it. There is a harmony in the balance of nature, which we all can find if we look for it. We all can transform in some way. Sometimes when transformation occurs the changes are so great that there is not a lot left of the original self. And that is fine because everyone should find a way to bloom and live an authentic life of purpose.

There is no one right or wrong way to decide on how to transform. It needs to be what is right for each person. This is a personal journey that is specific to the unique individual.

One must look within to start; soul searching for the answers about life and purpose. Looking within may seem daunting at first and be painful at times. Transformation can begin at any age.

Crying and emotions may come through. Disappointment, sadness, and resentment are emotions that can come out by looking within. Don't be afraid because it is okay to release the dam of emotions. Release with tears or screams. Let it be an internal cleansing that washes away the first layer of many more to come. Many life-changing decisions will come out of this time of reflection.

But what does inner wisdom really mean? Inner wisdom, to me, is connecting to our higher self that also connects to the source of our faith, spirituality, or a religious belief.

To me it is like a compass that helps direct me to stay on the right path in life. We get the answers we need and find comfort, safety and peace in feeling this connection. It is a beautiful experience when you learn to connect to it.

Inner wisdom will always help find the answers within. It will help find what is missing in life. Sometimes too much time is spent on living a life that is approved by others. But isn't our own approval really the most important one? The internal struggle starts when we ignore our inner wisdom.

Why is the inner wisdom ignored? We may not always listen to it because our mind is full of stress, worry, and anxiousness. The distractions of worry, money, and oither stresses blocks the inner wisdom from getting through. We need to learn to relax the mind, decrease the stress, and get to a calm place to be able to hear the inner wisdom.

Success can be determined by finances, jobs, and possessions, but is that really success and what brings happiness? Living a life disconnected from the inner wisdom and a true purpose can lead to internal conflicts that play in the background.

Stress, anger, lack of satisfaction, and an unbalanced life can be signs of living an unauthentic life. Transformation can bring an easier, happier, more satisfying life.

Inner wisdom is often ignored and pushed away. Just because it is not tangible does not mean it does not exist. We all have tapped into it at one time or another. Just like a rare pearl that is tucked in a beautiful oyster, we need to dig within to find this treasure.

I found it through hypnosis, but there are many ways to tap into it. Some techniques include religious practice, hypnosis, meditation, being quiet, yoga, therapy, or journaling.

Answers and connections don't happen overnight. We need to peel away to go deep and find the oyster. Journaling is great place to begin. By journaling you write about experiences, dreams, hopes, and fears.

There is no correct or absolute way to journal. Just start writing. Start with 15 minutes a day and increase the time to what is comfortable. The main thing is to get into the habit of journaling. Write about being happy, sad, frustrated, favorite things to do, hobbies, passions, trips, relationships, goals, successes, problems, and whatever comes to mind. Just let the writing flow easily.

Over time, writing will bring answers. More and more a deep connection with the inner self evolves easily and naturally when journaling. The conscious mind shuts down and allows the connection to go deep within to the subconscious and super conscious. The super conscious connects to your inner wisdom and can be found through journaling.

Look for patterns and thoughts that are negative or limiting beliefs. Look for passions. Then create a plan to start the process of transformation.

Create the plan and create an outline of steps and ways to execute it. Communicate to partners in life about the plan for change and talk about creating a happier life together. Create the buds on the tree that gradually grow. The main thing is to take the first step in the right direction and move forward towards a transformation to a balanced and happy life.

There are many road signs to help guide people on the journey in life. It is important to be aware and open to receive these signs. It could be something someone says, or read at just the right time, a song on the radio, or the car battery dying. Be open to the signs that come in many forms and in many ways.

Many times people miss the road signs of life and don't connect to the message. Take the steps to transform into the vibrant cherry blossom and live an authentic life.

Mary Battaglia is a Certified Clinical Hypnosis Practitioner and founder of Metro Hypnosis Center in Oradell, NJ. Mary is passionate about hypnosis and how it can help people peal away the fears and blocks that stops people from living their true life.

www.metrohypnosiscenter.com

TRANSITION

Life is one big transition.

– Willie Stargell

CHAPTER 31

CHOOSING IN THE NOW, MOMENT BY MOMENT

BY HARRIET CABELLY

"Everything can be taken from a man but one thing; the last of the human freedoms — to choose one's attitude in any given set of circumstances, to choose one's own way." Viktor Frankl

This quote, along with much of Viktor Frankl's writings in his book, *Man's Search for Meaning*, was transformational for me way back when I read it for the first time; it's been even more impactful throughout the years as I've gone through my life challenges. Like a GPS, it's recalibrated to keep me on a paved road as circumstances had periodically led me off the straight and easy path.

Since I was a teenager I've been fascinated by how some people seem to deal and live well despite their difficult circumstances that have seemingly befallen them. Hence my life's theme, and of more recently, my life's work, of "journeying" with people through their adversities towards rebuilding their life with renewed meaning and joy.

Lots of "stuff" happens to us throughout our lives. We all get hit with various struggles and difficulties. Nobody gets by unscathed. Therefore the real issue in how we live our lives is not so much what happens to us but rather how we respond to what happens and what we make of it.

When we see people with horrible circumstances who can be upbeat and positive, and then we see those who (seemingly) have it all and they're sour, bitter, and whiney, there's clearly something else at play here. It is not simply circumstance.

Sonja Lyubomirsky, psychologist and researcher in the field of happiness, came up with a pie chart representation showing the three main determinants of happiness and well being: 50% being genetics, 40% our behavior-our intentional activities which includes our attitude, and lo and behold, 10 percent circumstance.

We are obviously pre-disposed to a certain set-point of satisfaction irrespective of situations, due to our genetic make-up. Basic personality traits, nature, and temperament play out here.

But yet, after getting over the surprise that circumstance plays such a small role in our overall happiness, we can hone in on the idea that there is much we can do for ourselves to live well despite. It's within our purview to take responsibility and shed that victim-like mentality. We have control over what we do, over what and how we choose. We do not have to succumb to circumstance. "Man's inner strength may raise him above his outward fate." (Frankl)

This all may mean some work on our part. Life deserves a lot from us since we've been given the blessed chance to be here. With 40 percent in our pocket, we can create something pretty awesome. We can build up lots of muscle so that when the inevitable tough times come, we have the resilience to weather the storm, to cope and bounce back with renewed meaning and purpose.

It's all about choice, choosing in the now, moment by moment. Do we set up that negative spiral by maintaining a scowl on our face or do we smile and say hello to someone? It's a choice, in that moment. Do we automatically honk at the guy in front of us at the green light or do we take a breath and wait that extra second so that we're actually calming ourselves down and not reacting on auto-pilot? There's a domino effect to any choice we make. Our responses can put us on that upward spiral or the downward one. Small actions can make big differences in the quality of our lives.

So how can we optimize and enhance this almost half of our life's pie – this 40 percent that is in our power? We first have to decide that we want to get rid of those big nails on which we hang our hats of excuses for maintaining the status quo and holding onto our issues.

Once we make that decision to become creators of our lives, we then take an active role in bringing in more of the good and in strengthening our positive attitudinal muscle.

How do we do this?

The field of positive psychology studies how we can raise the bar of the quality of our life by utilizing strengths and focusing on what works. There are many applicable concepts that can be pulled in here to help us in our 40 percent work. Let's look at four strategies we can all begin to implement. Although they may seem simple and obvious, as Voltaire says, "Common sense is not so common."

BENEFIT-FINDER/FAULT-FINDER

What do we focus on? Do we hone in on the beautiful red rose or the thorns around it? We can't ignore the thorns (faults) because that's reality and we don't want to get hurt; but do we just complain about the prickly thorns and miss out on really seeing that gorgeous flower?

When it rains, can we look at it and instead of sulking, point out to our kids, " yes, it's disappointing we can't go on that picnic, but today the plants, trees, and grass are getting well fed. Let's have an indoor picnic."

Even in a lousy situation, can we glean a silver lining? Can we mine for some nuggets of gold? As Tal Ben-Shahar, positive psychology researcher and psychologist states, "Things don't necessarily happen for the best, but some people are able to make the best of things that happen."

GROWTH MINDSET

Are we open to learning new things and to improving? Do we believe that our abilities are not fixed; that our potential is limitless and we can keep opening up and expanding ourselves if we step outside our comfort zone? This mind-set is one of exhilaration, stimulation and passion as there is no such thing as boredom here. There is always newness in the ordinary. Again, it's how we see things, it's what we focus on, and it's how we choose to view things.

The field of neuro-plasticity is showing us that our brain can restructure itself with practice and training and it can continue to grow and change. This is a remarkably hopeful area of study as it basically teaches us that with work and time, we can grow new neurons and strengthen our mind muscles. We can therefore become more positive and more resilient.

APPRECIATE

There are two definitions of appreciation. One includes the idea of being grateful and the other is to grow in value. As Dr.Ben-Shahar says, "When we appreciate the good, the good appreciates." When we take for granted the good aspects of our life, it falls by the wayside; the good depreciates. But when we focus on the good and actively feel grateful, like the domino effect, we get more of it. Our eyes, and mind, are open to noticing more of the good. Again, it's what we {choose} to focus on.

Gratitude has been shown to enhance our health, optimism, generosity ,and overall well-being. As Oprah says, "What you focus on expands and when you focus on the goodness in your life, you create more of it. Opportunities, relationships, even money, flowed my way when I learned to be grateful no matter what happened in my life."

The Three Blessings is wonderful gratitude exercise by Martin Seligman, father of positive psychology, simple and powerful. Each night at bedtime, write down three things you're grateful for that day. They can be as simple as sitting with your hands around that beautiful mug of delicious coffee or being there for a friend in need, to nailing that job or getting that long-overdue promotion. Doing this exercise for 30 days straight begins to train the mind to seek out the good and then really feel it.

HAPPINESS BOOSTERS

Small bits of joy can awaken us. We may only be able to grab a few minutes during a day to bring a bit of pleasure into our life but once again, a little can go a long way. Smelling that lavender oil before bed and writing in one's journal (or doing the gratitude exercise) can become a positive bedtime routine, one to even look forward to.

Creating a small space with things that are meaningful to us can make us feel good when we enter and stay a while in that room. What are we bringing into our lives moment by moment? It's not about waiting for that big When but rather making those constant choices bit by bit. We can then string together the meaningful and joyful links, large and small, and create that colorful tapestry of life.

How we live is how we choose to live; what we bring into our life, what we focus on, what we savor, how we utilize our unlimited potential. Forty percent is not small potatoes. We have a lot of open space to paint a vibrant masterpiece known as our life. We then create a rich life; not exclusive of the bad, but where pain and joy stand tall and strongly entwined, nourishing one another's parts to build that one solid foundation of life.

Harriet Cabelly is a social worker and life coach with an emphasis in positive psychology. Harriet specializes in critical life transitions/issues and grief work and assists people on their journey of rebuilding their life through and beyond their adversities. She presents to various groups on different topics incorporating the life skills of well-being.

www.rebuildlifenow.com

CONTRIBUTING AUTHORS

Mary Battaglia

Jude Bijou, M.A., M.F.T.

Harriett Cabelly

Caryn Chow

Amy Connelley

Roxanne D'Angelo

Ed Gaelick, CLU, ChFC

Renee Gambino

Julie Genovese

Joseph P. Ghabi, M.S.

Steve Goodier

Laci Greer

Denise Hansard

Alexandra Harra

Carmen Harra, Ph.D.

Joan Herrmann

Susan Hickman, Ph.D., Psy.D.

Ruschelle Khanna, LCSW

Linzi Levinson

Trace Levinson

Suzanne Trenzia Moore

Caryn O'Sullivan

Richard Perro

Heidi Ravis, Ed.M., LMHC

Barbara Rubel, M.A., BCETS

Ann Sheybani

Shannon Sennefelder

Mary Ila Ward

Jennifer Weggmen, M.A.

Michelle Welch

Fern Weis

Debra Wilber

CPSIA information can be obtained at www.ICGtesting.com
Printed in the USA
BVOW06s1527120116

432406BV00002B/113/P